Gospel Lesson Plans

by
Catherine Geary Uhl

PAULIST PRESS
New York/Ramsey/Toronto

ACKNOWLEDGMENTS

Reprinted by permission:

The chorus of "Let Heaven Rejoice" is reprinted by permission of North American Liturgy Resources, 2110 West Peo-
ria Avenue, Phoenix, Arizona 85029. All rights reserved.

"The Spirit of the Lord" by Jim Strathdee. Copyright ©
1969 by Jim Strathdee. Used with permission.

Library of Congress
Catalog Card Number: 79-65918

ISBN: 0-8091-2211-1

Published by Paulist Press
Editorial Office: 1865 Broadway, New York, N.Y. 10023
Business Office: 545 Island Road, Ramsey, N.J. 07446

Printed and bound in the
United States of America

CONTENTS

How to Use This Book

Each lesson begins with a simple statement to the teacher giving the aim.

All lessons consist of a simplified story of the Sunday gospel, with a practical application to the student's life found in the Activity; Psalm and Liturgy; Letter to the Parents; and questions for the teacher to use as a guide. Possible new words for your students are followed by a simplified meaning in parentheses.

Activity:
Is an experience to reinforce the lesson. It should be used where it is most effective for that particular lesson. Each lesson suggests where the author feels it is most effective. But you know your students best; therefore, change the format to be most meaningful to your class.

Responsorial Psalm:
Is included in the liturgy and is worded as it appears in the Sunday Mass. If the wording is difficult for your students, explain it, but do not change it. Repeat it as often as you feel is necessary. We want the students to recognize it when they hear it at Mass.

Liturgy:
Should be a practical application of the lesson from the gospel.

Have an altar or prayer table in the classroom. On it have the Bible opened to today's lesson. Have two lighted candles, unless the lesson specifies a change. Let the students set up the altar each week. Occasionally, bring flowers and encourage the students to bring something for the altar.

Letter to the Parents:
This is very important. The student will retain more if the parents reinforce the lesson at home throughout the week.

Before the first class of the year, send home a letter explaining that a letter to parents will be sent home each week. (Suggested letter on this page.)

Supplies Needed and Patterns:
Supplies needed are listed at the beginning of each lesson. This gives the teacher time to get the necessary supplies prepared ahead. Call on volunteers for this. Patterns follow the lessons.

Ordo:
At the beginning of the year, with your parish priest, check the Ordo. This will tell you: (1) which Sunday of the liturgical year you will be starting your classes; (2) the number of Sundays between Christmas and Lent; (3) the number of Sundays after Easter; (4) the number of Sundays of the year until your classes close for summer vacation.

The First and Last Class of Each Year:
First class should allow time for everyone to get acquainted.

Last class should always include a joy celebration—a happy time for the year we spent together.

Letter to Be Sent to Parents before the First Class of the School Year:
Dear Parents,

We are happy to welcome   (child's name) to our class.

This year, the lessons will be based on the Sunday gospels. You can help us teach your child by reinforcing the lesson at home throughout the week.

We will send home a note each week suggesting ways to reinforce the gospel in your child's life. Together, you and your child will grow in the love and knowledge of God.

Feel free to call on us at anytime if you have any questions.

Sincerely in Christ,
Teacher _____
Telephone

Instructions For Making and Using Matching Cards

To Make:
Count the number of words to be used.

You will need to double this number.

Rule tag board or poster board to size desired for the cards. Do NOT cut apart.

Or draw number of shapes needed for matching cards. See patterns that correspond to lesson.

With pencil, print lightly two cards for each word.

With felt pen, trace penciled lettering. Use same color for same word, but different colors for different words. (This enables the non-reader to participate.)

Cut out.

Cover both sides of each card with clear adhesive shelf paper.

To Use:
Teacher or helper places one set of cards on table in their proper sequence, reading them aloud as he/she does so.

With the second set turned face down, students select cards.

Students match their cards to cards on table, as the teacher reads words again in their proper sequence.

When cards have all been matched, one student, who can read, reads cards aloud and class repeats.

Individual sets may be made, so each student has one and works with a teacher's aide in above manner.

After matching cards have been used in a lesson, keep them available as review or for students who arrive early to use before class.

Suggested Pictures to Use With Gospel Stories

Twenty-third Sunday of Year
Cycle B—Jesus cures the deaf man.
Twenty-fourth Sunday of Year
Cycle C—The Good Shepherd.
Twenty-fifth Sunday of Year
Cycle A—Workers in the vineyard.
Twenty-sixth Sunday of Year
Cycle C—Rich man and Lazarus the beggar.
Twenty-eighth Sunday of Year
Cycle A—Parable of the wedding feast (not Cana).
Cycle B—The rich young man.
Cycle C—Cure of ten lepers.
Twenty-ninth Sunday of Year
Cycle A—Tribute to Caesar.
Cycle C—Woman who pesters judge.
Thirtieth Sunday of Year
Cycle B—Jesus cures the blind beggar.
Cycle C—The Publican and the Pharisee.
Thirty-first Sunday of Year
Cycle C—Zacchaeus.
Thirty-second Sunday of Year
Cycle B—Widow's mite.
Thirty-fourth Sunday of Year
Cycle A—Christ the King.
Cycle B—Jesus before Pilate.
Cycle C—Jesus and the two thieves on the cross.
First Sunday of Advent—Cycles A-B-C
Jesus preaching.
Second Sunday of Advent—Cycles A-B-C
John the Baptist preaching or baptizing the people.
Third Sunday of Advent—Cycles A-B-C
John the Baptist preaching or baptizing the people.
Fourth Sunday of Advent
Cycle A—Mary and Joseph.
Cycle B—Annunciation.
Cycle C—Visitation.
First Sunday of Year—Cycles A-B-C
Baptism of Jesus.
Second Sunday of Year
Cycle A—Baptism of Jesus—Present-day Baptism.
Cycle C—Marriage feast at Cana.
Third Sunday of Year
Cycle B—Jesus calling Peter and Andrew to follow him.
Cycle C—Jesus reading the scroll in the synagogue.
Fourth Sunday of Year
Cycle A—Sermon on the Mount.
Cycle C—Jesus reading the scroll in the synagogue.

Fifth Sunday of Year
Cycle B—Jesus praying (not the Agony in the Garden).
Cycle C—The large catch of fish.
Sixth Sunday of Year
Cycle B—Jesus cures a leper.
Cycle C—Sermon on the Mount.
Seventh Sunday of Year
Cycle B—Jesus cures a paralytic let down through the roof.
Ninth Sunday of Year
Cycle A—House built on a rock; house built on sand.
Cycle C—Curing the Centurion's servant.
Tenth Sunday of Year
Cycle A—Jesus calls Matthew.
Cycle B—Jesus' mother and relatives wait outside.
Cycle C—Curing the son of widow of Naim.
Eleventh Sunday of Year
Cycle B—Picture of a tree or large bush.
Cycle C—Woman washing Jesus' feet with her tears.
First Sunday of Lent—Cycles A-B-C
Jesus is tempted.
Second Sunday of Lent—Cycles A-B-C
Transfiguration.
Third Sunday of Lent
Cycle A—Woman at the well.
Cycle B—Driving the money changers from the temple.
Fourth Sunday of Lent
Cycle A—Curing the man born blind.
Cycle C—Prodigal son.
Fifth Sunday of Lent
Cycle A—Jesus raises Lazarus.
Cycle C—Woman caught in adultery.
Palm Sunday—Cycles A-B-C
Passion of our Lord.
Second Sunday of Easter—Cycles A-B-C
Doubting Thomas.
Third Sunday of Easter
Cycle A—Road to Emmaus; Crucifixion; Resurrection.
Fourth Sunday of Easter—Cycles A-B-C
Good Shepherd.
Cycle A—Children and their pets.
Fifth Sunday of Easter
Cycle C—Last Supper.

Cycle A

Cycle A
First Sunday of Advent

Always Be Ready To Meet Jesus

Supplies Needed
styrofoam wreath
3 purple, 1 rose colored candles (4
white if colors are not available)
sharp knife to cut styrofoam
evergreen cuttings
purple ribbon (1 yard)
straight pins
matches

Activity
Make an Advent wreath. Use a styrofoam wreath. Cut holes to insert 4 candles. Cover styrofoam with evergreens. Tie in place with purple ribbon. Pin ribbon so it won't slip as you wind it. Use in liturgy during Advent. First week light 1 candle; second week, 2; third week, 3; the third candle lit is the rose colored one, a sign of hope. Light all candles the last week. When complete, place on altar in prayer corner. As you are making the wreath, involve the children and talk about preparing to meet Christ.

While we are preparing during Advent to meet Jesus at Christmas, we should always be preparing to meet Jesus when we die.

Discuss
Sunday Advent begins. Advent is the time of the year in which the Church prepares to meet Jesus at his birth [Christmas]. It is time for us to prepare to meet Jesus also. How do we prepare to meet Jesus? [By being good.]

Lesson
One day Jesus told his followers this: If the owner of the house knew when the thief was coming, he would keep a watchful eye and not allow his house to be broken into. Then Jesus said: You must be ready in the same way. You never know when the Son of Man is coming. Jesus often calls himself the Son of Man. He was telling his followers that they did not know when he would call them to heaven. Jesus tells us also that we do not know when we will die and meet Jesus; therefore, we should always be ready to meet Jesus. [While we are preparing during Advent to meet Jesus at Christmas, we should always be preparing to meet Jesus when we die.]

Liturgy
Gather around altar. Light one candle on the Advent wreath. Join hands.

All:

(say with joy) I rejoiced when I heard them say: Let us go to the house of the Lord.

Sing:
"O Come, Emmanuel," if the students know it or select a Christmas carol they all know.

All:
I rejoiced when I heard them say: Let us go to the house of the Lord.

Letter to Parents
Dear Parents,

Advent is the time of preparation for the celebration of Christ's birth, but we must always be prepared to meet Christ.

Attached are instructions for making an Advent wreath. Use as a centerpiece at the family meal or at family prayer time.

Note to Teacher
Attach a copy of Advent wreath instructions from the Activity to the parents' letter.

Questions
What special day is Christmas? (Jesus' birthday.)
How do we prepare to meet Jesus? (By being good.)
When will Jesus come for us again? (When we die.)
Should we always be ready to meet Jesus?

Cycle A
Second Sunday of Advent

John the Baptist Preaches "Repent"

Supplies Needed
Advent wreath
matching cards (See instructions, page 2; words for cards in Activity.)

Lesson
John the baptizer was teaching people in the desert. He said, "Reform your lives." [That means start to be a better person.] Then he added, "The reign of God is at hand." That was his was of saying Jesus was coming.

Many people were sorry for all the wrong they had ever done and were baptized in the river.

When the people were baptized, that was their way of showing their sorrow and saying they wanted to do better in the future. How do we show our sorrow? Do we say "I am sorry"? To whom do we say "I am sorry"? Do we also tell God we are sorry?

Activity
Matching cards.

When I say I am sorry, God forgives me.

Liturgy
Gather around altar. Light 2 candles of the Advent wreath. Close eyes and bow heads. Teacher (quietly): God sees into our hearts. He knows everything that is there. In your heart, tell God you are sorry for ever doing anything wrong. (Pause.)

Teacher:
Feel God's peace inside your heart. (Pause.)

All:
Justice shall flourish in his time, and fullness of peace forever.

Sing:
"Thank You, God" from "Hi God" record. "Praise God" to tune "Amazing Grace." Repeat the words "Praise God" throughout song.

Letter to Parents
Dear Parents,
Today we talked about repentance and took time to feel God's peace within us after saying "I am sorry." Pause quietly in your family prayer to feel God's peace. End your prayer time with a greeting of peace.
Sincerely in Christ,
Teacher _____

Questions
How do we show our sorrow? (By saying, "I am sorry.") To whom do we say, "I am sorry"? (God and anyone we have offended.)

Cycle A
Third Sunday of Advent

Jesus Is Our Savior We Love Him

Supplies Needed
Advent wreath
3″×5″ lined index card, at top type: "Present to giver for redemption"
scissors
glue
gift wrap envelopes (see pattern, page 7)

Lesson
Last week we heard about John the Baptist telling the people to repent. He baptized the people who were sorry for their wrongs. Now some men did not like to be told they were doing wrong, so they had John put in jail. While John was in jail, he sent some of his friends to Jesus to ask him, "Are you he who is to come or do we look for another?" (He was asking Jesus if he was the savior, the one who was to save us.) Jesus said, "Tell John what you hear and see; the blind see again; cripples walk; deaf hear; dead men are raised to life and the poor have the good news preached [taught] to them. Blest is the man who finds no stumbling block in me." By that Jesus meant, "Blest is the man who loves me and accepts me as I am."

Activity
Have students print on slips of paper special things they can do for other family members. Example: Set table so brother or sister can do their homework. Make one for each family member. Wrap in gift envelope for under the Christmas tree. Student will do whatever the slip says when family member returns it to be redeemed. (See pattern for gift envelope, page 7.)

Liturgy
Gather around altar. Light 3 candles on Advent wreath.

All:
Lord, we love you. You are our savior. (Raise hands high.) Lord, come and save us.

Letter to Parents
Dear Parents,
  Jesus, our Savior, is coming. In your family prayer, include the psalm "Lord, Come and Save Us."

Sincerely in Christ,
Teacher _____

Questions
Jesus is our Savior.
What does Savior mean? (One who saves.)
Jesus died to save us.
Because we are saved can we go to heaven?

Cycle A
Fourth Sunday of Advent

Jesus Is Our Savior

Supplies Needed
cardboard crib scene or crèche
12 popsickle sticks per student
glue
small Christ Child for each student

Discuss
We have been talking in our last few classes about being sorry for our sins and God will forgive us. In today's story the angel tells Joseph to name Mary's baby "Jesus because he will save his people from their sins."

Lesson
This is how the birth of Jesus came about. When his mother Mary was engaged to Joseph, she was with child by the power of the Holy Spirit. Joseph was worried, when sud-

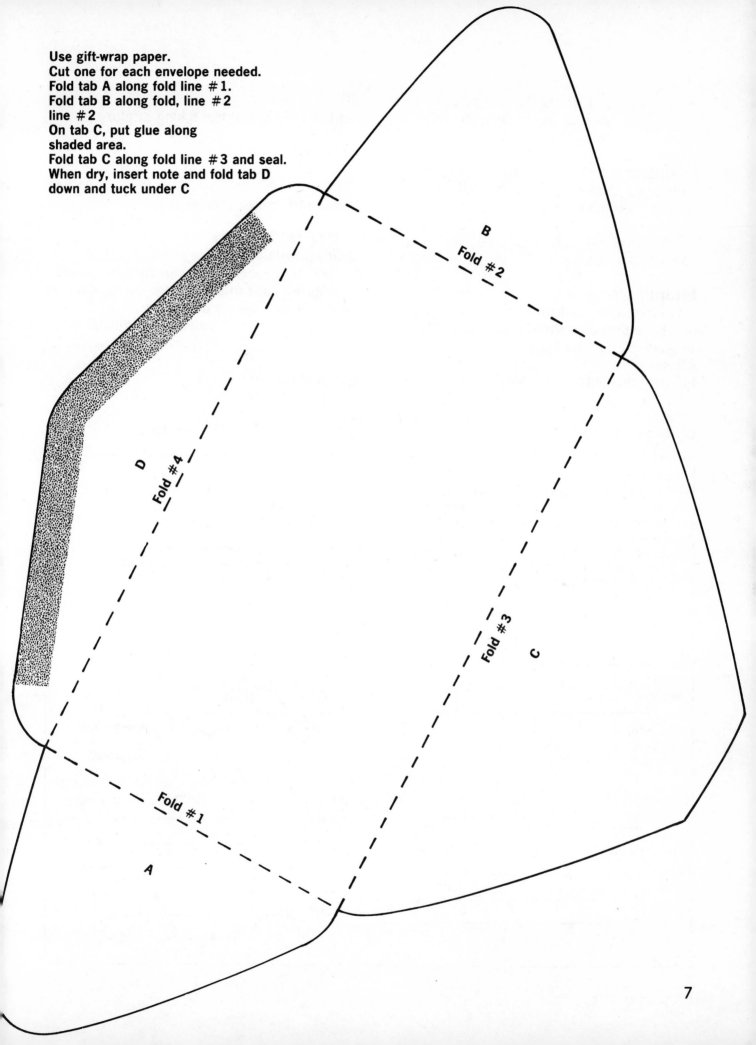

Use gift-wrap paper.
Cut one for each envelope needed.
Fold tab A along fold line #1.
Fold tab B along fold, line #2
line #2
On tab C, put glue along
shaded area.
Fold tab C along fold line #3 and seal.
When dry, insert note and fold tab D
down and tuck under C

B
Fold #2

D
Fold #4

Fold #3
C

Fold #1

A

7

denly the angel of the Lord appeared in a dream and said to him: "Joseph, have no fear about taking Mary as your wife. It is by the Holy Spirit that she has conceived this child. She is to have a son and you are to name him Jesus because he will save his people from their sins."

Stress: Are we Jesus' people? Did Jesus come to save us?

Liturgy
If crib has been put up in church, go to it. If not, have crib on altar in classroom.

All:
Let the Lord enter; he is king of glory.

Sing:
Christmas carols.

All:
Let the Lord enter; He is king of glory.

Activity
Make popsickle stick crib.

(See instructions, this page.)

Letter to Parents
Dear Parents,
Light all 4 candles on your Advent wreath.
Include "Let the Lord enter; He is King of Glory" in your family prayer this week.
Sincerely in Christ,
Teacher _____

Questions
Are we Jesus' people?
Did Jesus come to save us?
Is Savior another name for Jesus?

CRIB DIRECTIONS
1. Lay 4 popsickle sticks as shown in Fig. 1.
2. Repeat Fig. 1 using 4 additional popsickle sticks. (Avoid warped sticks.)
3. Glue 1 stick to right side of each set of 4 as shown in Fig. 2. Be sure stick is in from ends at least the width of 1 stick.
4. Glue second stick close to left edge as possible on each set of 4 as shown in Fig. 3.
5. When dry enough to handle, put 2 parts together with legs on outside; flat surface to inside.
6. Put glue on bottom edge and hold until set. This takes patience. See Fig. 4.

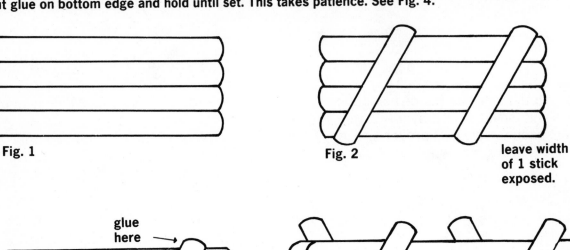

Fig. 1

Fig. 2

leave width of 1 stick exposed.

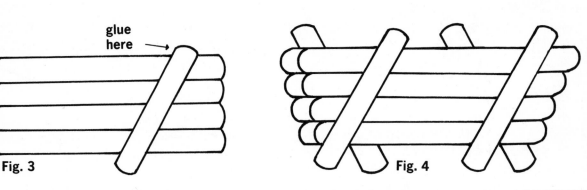

glue here →

Fig. 3

Fig. 4

Cycle A
First Sunday of Year

John Obeys Jesus; We Obey

Supplies Needed
poster board (1 sheet)
magazines
scissors
glue
slips of paper, lined
pencils

Lesson
Jesus came to where John was baptizing people by the Jordan river, and told John to baptize him. John tried to refuse [Say "No"]. John said, "I should be baptized by you, yet you come to me." Jesus answered, "Give in for now. We must do this if we would fulfill all of God's demands." So John gave in.

Discuss
Jesus told John to baptize him. John didn't want to, but did because Jesus told him to.

Liturgy
Have students print "I will obey" on slips of paper. Gather around altar. Make up a prayer telling Jesus we will try to be good. Each student places his or her paper on the altar and says own prayer as they do so. After each student's prayer, all say: **The Lord will bless his people with peace.**

Activity
Talk about other ways in which we are good. Make a collage of people being good by being helpful.

Letter to Parents
Dear Parents,
Today we talked about obeying and helping others. Encourage your child with praise whenever they help others and obey willingly.
Sincerely in Christ,
Teacher _____

Questions
Did John want to baptize Jesus?
Did John obey Jesus?
Do we obey?

Cycle A
Second Sunday of Year

I Am A Child of God; God Is My Father

Supplies Needed
dove-shaped matching cards
(see Activity and pattern, page 10)
basin or bowl of water
(large mixing bowl)
pitcher of water
paper towels
potted plant to water

Review
Use collage to stimulate recall. Discuss last week's story of Jesus' baptism. Fill in parts students fail to remember, then add:

Lesson
When John told about baptizing Jesus, John said, "I saw the Spirit descend like a dove from the sky and come to rest on him." Then John added, "This is God's chosen one."

John was telling the people that Jesus is God's son. We have been baptized also. At our baptism God made us his children. Jesus is our brother.

Activity
Have everyone wash their hands. As all wash, explain: **In baptism the priest poured water on us as a symbol [sign] of washing us clean of any wrong before God.**

Water potted plant. At same time, explain: **Water is also a symbol [sign] of our new life as God's child. Just as the water we put on the plant is necessary for its life.**

Liturgy

Visit baptistry and thank God for making us his children. End visit by all saying: Here I am, Lord, I come to do your will.

Activity

Matching cards (dove-shaped)—pattern below.

Instructions to make and use, page 2.

At baptism I became a child of God. God is my father.

Letter to Parents

Dear Parents,

Today we learned that at Baptism we became children of God. Jesus is our brother. In your family prayer, include a prayer of thanks to God for making your family his children.

Sincerely in Christ,
Teacher —————

Questions

Did I become a child of God at Baptism?
Is Jesus my brother?
Is God my Father?

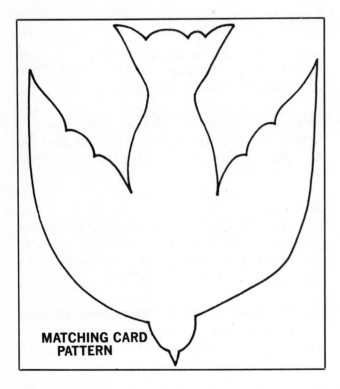

MATCHING CARD PATTERN

We Let Our Light Shine For Others to See

Supplies Needed

poster board (1 sheet)
magazines
glue
scissors
candles on altar

Lesson

When Jesus heard that John had been arrested, Jesus went to Galilee. He began to tell the people, "Reform your lives [begin to be better people], the kingdom of heaven is at hand." [He was telling the people that he had come to save them, but many did not understand him.]

Liturgy

Gather around altar. Light candles.
(Explain salvation: Jesus came to save us.)

All:

The Lord is my light and my salvation.

Sing:

"This Little Light of Mine."
This little light of mine, I'm gonna let it shine. (repeat 3 times)
Let it shine. (repeat 3 times)

Teacher:

We let our light shine by being better people as Jesus told us.

Discuss

Ways we can be better people. Ask how students help at home, work or school. Encourage them to think of new ways to help. Talk about being a better person by being courteous and cheerful. When we are cheerful and smile, we are letting our light shine for others to see.

Activity
Make a collage of happy faces of people from old magazines.

Letter to Parents
Dear Parents,

Our psalm is: The Lord Is My Light and My Salvation. We let our light shine for others to see by being cheerful and courteous. Encourage these qualities in your child. Include the psalm in your family prayers this week.

Sincerely in Christ,
Teacher _____

Questions
The light of Jesus is in us.
How do we let our light shine for others to see?

Cycle A
Fourth Sunday of Year

Apply the Beatitudes to Our Life

Supplies Needed
collage of last week
matching cards (see Activity)
paper with printed matching
cards sayings (1 per student)

Review
Use collage from last class.

Sing: "This Little Light of Mine."

Teacher: What did we learn last week? How do we let our light shine for others to see? (By wearing a cheerful, happy face.)

Lesson
In today's story about Jesus, he tells us more ways to let our little light shine for others to see. One day Jesus told the people:

Blest are the poor in spirit [people who are not stuck up] for they will go to heaven.

Blest are the lowly [kind people] for they shall own the land.

Blest are the sorrowing [sad] for they shall be comforted [made happy].

Blest are they who hunger and thirst for holiness [try to be fair to others] for they shall have their fill.

Blest are they who show mercy [people who forgive others] for others will forgive them.

Blest are the single-hearted [those who do good] for they shall see God.

Blest are the peace makers [those who help others to be friends] for they shall be called sons of God.

Blest are those persecuted for holiness' sake [are teased for being good] for the Kingdom of Heaven is theirs.

Stress: Take each beatitude one at a time and discuss it.
Jesus was telling us we should let our light shine. Let us repeat the ways:
Be kind to others.
Be fair with others.
Forgive others.
Do good to others.
Help others be friends.
We must not be stuck up [love everyone].
When we are sad, tell Jesus [pray].
Know people will tease us for being good.

Liturgy
Gather around altar. Join hands.

All:
Happy are the poor in spirit, the Kingdom of Heaven is theirs.

Sing:
"This Little Light of Mine."

All:
Happy are the poor in spirit, the Kingdom of Heaven is theirs.

Activity
Matching cards.

Be kind	Help others
Be fair	Love others
Forgive	Love Jesus
Do good	Pray

(These can be used as an examination of conscience by asking: Am I kind? Am I fair? Do I forgive? etc.

Letter to Parents
Dear Parents,

Today we learned about the beatitudes. Your child is bringing home a simplified version of them for the family bulletin board or to hang in his/her room. Read them with your child several times this week. They can be used as an examination of conscience by asking:

Am I fair?	*Do I do good?*
Am I kind?	*Do I help others?*
Do I forgive?	*Do I love others?*
Do I love Jesus?	*Do I pray?*

This examination is to help us to be a better person, not to prepare us for the Sacrament of Reconciliation.

Sincerely in Christ,
Teacher _____

Questions
Name some ways we let our light shine.
Be kind to others.
Be fair with others.
Forgive others.
Do good to others.
Help others be friends.
Love others.
Love Jesus.
Pray.

Cycle A
Fifth Sunday of Year

We Let Our Light Shine
For All to See the Goodness of Our Acts

Supplies Needed
1 votive candle per student
1 large candle
beads, sequins
glitter
scissors
straight pins
glue
construction paper

Activity
Have each student decorate a votive candle. Use old beads and sequins. Attach to candle with pins. Or use glue and glitter. Glue or pin bits of construction paper cut in flower shapes. While working, sing, "This Little Light of Mine." Have 1 large candle and everyone add some decoration to it. When complete, place on altar with Bible.

Lesson
One day Jesus said to his disciples [friends]: "You are the light of the world. Men do not light a lamp, then put it under a basket. They set it on a stand where it gives light to all the house. In the same way, your light must shine before men so that they may see the goodness in your acts and give praise to your Heavenly Father."

[Who is our Heavenly Father?]

[How does Jesus say our light must shine? So others see our goodness.]

Liturgy
Gather around altar. Light the large candle. Join hands.

All:
The just man is a light in the darkness to the upright.

Sing:
"This Little Light of Mine."

Teacher:
Our light must shine so others may see the goodness in our acts and give praise to our Heavenly Father.

Sing:
"Praise God" to the tune "Amazing Grace." (Repeat words "Praise God" throughout song.

Letter to Parents
Dear Parents,

Today your child is bringing home a candle decorated by him/her in class. Let it burn during your family prayer time. When your child lights it, say, "Our light must shine so others see the goodness in our acts and give praise to our Heavenly Father."

Sincerely in Christ,
Teacher _____

Questions
Who is our heavenly Father?
How does Jesus say our light must shine?
(So others see the goodness of our acts.)

Cycle A
Sixth Sunday of Year

We Must Be Truly Good

Supplies Needed
Matching cards from Fourth Sunday of Year—Cycle A
Begin class by singing "This Little Light of Mine."

Lesson
One day Jesus spoke about the scribes and pharisees. They were people who *pretended* to be very holy [very good]. Jesus said to his disciples: "I tell you, unless your holiness [goodness] is greater than that of the scribes and pharisees, you shall not enter the kingdom of God [heaven]."

Discuss
Jesus was telling his disciples that it is by being good and holy that our light shines for others to see. We must be good and holy to get to heaven.

Activity
Use matching cards from 4th Sunday of year—A.

Liturgy
Gather around altar.

All:
Happy are they who follow the law of the Lord.

Teacher:
As I ask the following questions, keep your eyes closed and answer each question quietly in your heart. (Pause after each question.)
Am I kind?
Am I fair?
Do I forgive others?
Do I help others?
Do I try to be good?
Do I love other people?
Do I love Jesus? Let us pray:

All:
Happy are they who follow the law of the Lord.

Letter to Parents
Dear Parents,

In your family prayer time it is good to occasionally examine your conscience. With eyes closed, everyone remains quiet, while one person asks questions. Each question is

followed by a pause. Am I kind? Am I fair? Do I forgive? Do I help others? Do I try to be good? Do I love others? Do I love Jesus?
Sincerely in Christ,
Teacher _____

Questions
Did Jesus say we must be good?
Did Jesus say we must be holy?

Cycle A
Seventh Sunday of Year

Love Your Enemies

Supplies Needed
poster board (1 sheet)
magazines
scissors
glue

Lesson
Jesus said, "You have heard the commandment to love your countrymen but hate your enemies. My command to you is: Love your enemies, pray for those who do not like you. This will prove that you are a child of your Heavenly Father."

[This is not an easy thing Jesus told us to do. It is hard to love someone who does not like us. When we are with someone who does not like us, we should think: "Jesus loves me. Jesus also loves this person who does not like me. Jesus died so I can go to heaven. Jesus died so_____can go to heaven also."]

Activity
Make a collage of people expressing love through friendship and helping each other. When finished, place on the altar.

Liturgy
Gather around altar. Join hands and sing: "They'll Know We Are Christians." Quietly in your heart, say a prayer for those who do not like you.

All:
The Lord is kind and merciful.

Letter to Parents
Dear Parents,
Jesus' command was to love our enemies. This week in your family prayer, have each member say a silent prayer for anyone they find hard to like.
Sincerely in Christ,
Teacher _____

Questions
Did Jesus tell us to love those who do not like us?
Did Jesus tell us to pray for those who do not like us?

Cycle A
Eighth Sunday of Year

God, Our Father, Loves Us and Cares For Us

Supplies Needed
clear contact paper (2" squares)
35 mm slide frames
slide projector
permanent ink marking
pens (fine point)
glue

Activity
Make slides of birds, flowers and happy people of all ages. Directions: Students draw on contact paper: flowers; birds; and happy people. Remove paper from back of contact. Center in 35 mm slide frames following instructions on the package. Show slides as you tell today's gospel story.

Lesson

Jesus said to his disciples: "Do not worry about what you are to eat or drink or use for clothing. Look at the birds in the sky. They do not sow or reap [plant a garden], yet your Heavenly Father feeds them. Are not you more important than they? As for clothes, why worry? Learn a lesson from the way the wild flowers grow. They do not work. If God can clothe in such beauty the grass of the field, which blooms today and is thrown on the fire tomorrow, will he not give much more to you? Your Heavenly Father knows all that you need. Look first for his love and holiness and all these things will be given you besides."

Liturgy

Gather around altar. (If possible, have fresh flowers on the altar this week.)

All:

Rest in God alone, my soul.

(Have each student thank God for some special blessing.) After each, all repeat: Rest in God alone, my soul.

Letter to Parents

Dear Parents,

Today we heard the story of God's love and care for the birds of the air and the lillies of the field, yet how much more he loves us. In your family prayer this week, include the psalm: Rest in God Alone, My Soul.

Sincerely in Christ,
Teacher _____

Questions

Is God our Father?
Does God love us?
Does God care for us?
Does God love us more than the birds and flowers?

Cycle A
Ninth Sunday of Year

Jesus Wants Us to Be The Best Person We Can Be

Supplies Needed

flat rock, approximately 3″
in diameter (1 per student)
paint brushes
acrylic paints
child's block (2)
9″ x 13″ cake pan (2)
approximately 4 cups sand
pitcher
water

Activity

In a 9" x 13" cake pan, place a pile of sand, approximately 3 inches deep in the center, leaving the outer edge of the pan free of sand. Place a small block of wood on top of sand. (Child's building block will be excellent.) Have one student gently hold a finger on the building block. With a pitcher of water pour it so the sand washes from under the block. In another pan, have a large flat rock. Place a child's block on the rock. Again, pour water on the rock as one student gently holds the block. (You may want to do this experiment outdoors for it can get messy.)

Lesson

One day Jesus told his disciples, "None of those who cry Lord, Lord, will enter the kingdom of God [heaven], but only the one who does the will of my Father in heaven." [Jesus was saying, only those who do what God wants will get to heaven.]

Discuss

Can you name something God wants us to do? (Love God—love others—pray—be good, etc.) Discuss the following quote:

Anyone who hears my words and obeys them is like the wise man who built his house on a rock. When the rain and the winds came, his house remained standing. [Compare to block on rock in pan.] Anyone who hears my words and does not obey them is like the foolish man who built his house on the sand. When the rains came and the wind blew, the house fell down and was completely ruined. (Compare to block on sand in pan.)

Discuss
Jesus is like the rock in our experiment. We can depend on him. But we must do what he asks. (Review again the things God wants us to do.)

Liturgy
Gather around altar. Join hands.

All:
Lord, be my rock of safety. O Lord, I love you. Help me to love everyone. Today I will be the best person I can be. Lord, be my rock of safety.

Activity
Paint rocks. Have a flat rock about 3 inches in diameter. (Can be purchased at a building supply store or lumber yard.) One rock per student. Use acrylic paints. Encourage students to paint a cross or the word Jesus or both on their rock.

Letter to Parents
Dear Parents,
   This week, encourage your child to say the following prayer each morning as his/her morning offering: Lord, be my rock of safety. O Lord, I love you. Help me to love everyone. Today I will be the best person I can be. Lord, be my rock of safety.
                                    Sincerely in Christ,
                                    Teacher _____

Questions
Does Jesus love us?
Does Jesus want us to be our best?
Should we love everyone?

16

Cycle A
Tenth Sunday of Year

God Loves Us and Wants Us to Be Good

Supplies Needed
1 pre-punched sewing card per student
1 blunt tapestry needle per student
yarn 5 ft. long, per student (Have a variety of colors for students to choose from.)
Open lesson with prayer from last week.

Activity
Play a game of "Follow the Leader." Let more than one person have a turn at being the leader.

Lesson
One day Jesus saw a man named Matthew busy collecting taxes. Jesus said, "Follow me." Matthew got up and followed Jesus. Later Jesus was eating at Matthew's house. When the pharisees [leaders of the people] saw this, they complained to the disciples [Jesus' followers]: "Why is Jesus eating with tax collectors and those who break the law?" they asked. When Jesus heard them, he said, "People who are in good health do not need a doctor, sick people do. I have not come to call the just, but sinners."

Discuss
Jesus was saying that if everyone had always been good, he would not have had to come to save us. Because we are sinners, Jesus came to show us how to be good and to die for us. Jesus came to tell everyone all about God's great love for all people.

Liturgy
Gather around altar. Join hands.

All:
The upright [the good people] will show the saving power of God.

Teacher:
Jesus, you love us even when we do wrong.

All:
The upright will show the saving power of God.

Teacher:
God, our father, you love us with a great love.

All:
The upright will show the saving power of God.

Teacher:
Help us to be upright in all we do.

All:
The upright will show the saving power of God.

Activity:
Sewing card. God loves me. (See below).

Letter to Parents
Dear Parents,

God, our Father, loves us with a great love and wants us to be "upright" in all we do. Always be aware that everything you do, no matter how great or small, is an example to your child to follow. Our prayer today: The Upright Will Show the Saving Power of God.

Sincerely in Christ,
Teacher _____

Questions
Does God love us?
Did Jesus come to save us?
Does God want us to be good?

SEWING CARD PATTERN AND INSTRUCTIONS
1. Use cards from hosiery packages.
2. With a sharp tapestry needle, punch holes.
3. Draw lines for students to follow. Do steps 1, 2, and 3 prior to class.
4. Student uses blunt tapestry needle and 5 ft. of yarn to sew card.

Cycle A
Eleventh Sunday of Year

We Belong to God; We Give Willingly to Others

Supplies Needed
A gift package for each student. Have the same thing in each package, but wrap them all differently. No name tags on any of the gifts. (Suggest: a small statue of Jesus or a crucifix. Your church goods store has several inexpensive items.)

Activity
Have each student select a gift, but instruct the students not to open the gift at this time.

Lesson
Jesus often called the people his sheep. That is what he does in today's story. One day Jesus told his twelve Apostles [special followers] "Go after the lost sheep. Tell them 'The reign of God is at hand.'" [That was Jesus' way of saying he had come to save the people.] Then he told his apostles, "Cure the sick, raise the dead, heal the lepers and drive out the demons. The gift you have received, give as a gift."

Discuss
Jesus said, "The gift you have received, give as a gift." Let's all give our gift to someone else. (Be sure each student ends up with a gift but a different one than the one they first chose.) After this exchange, let the students open their gifts. If a student is reluctant to give his/her gift to another, say: "Jesus asked us to give the gifts we received to others. Sometime it is hard, but because Jesus asked us to, we do it."

After the gift exchange: "Jesus gave us a greater gift than the one we received today. He made us his people, the sheep of his flock."

Liturgy
Gather around altar.

All:
We are his people, the sheep of his flock. Care for us, O Lord, as the shepherd cares for his sheep. We are his people the sheep of his flock.

(Have one person read the Twenty-third Psalm while the rest of the class and teacher do the gestures.)
The Lord is my shepherd;
I shall not want.
    (Hands raised high—look up.)
In green [verdant] pastures
He gives me rest [repose]
    (Rest cheek on folded hands,
    close eyes.)
Beside restful waters he leads me;
he refreshes my soul
    (Join hands, teacher leads
    students around room.)
He guides me in right paths
for his name's sake.
    (Continue around room.)
Even though I walk in the dark
valley, I fear no evil; for you are at my side.
    (Stop, raise hands high, look up,
    bring right hand down to side, palm out.)
With your rod and your staff
that gives me courage.
    (Hold above position.)
You spread the table before me
in the sight of my foes.
    (Hands in front, palms down,
    hands slowly move opposite directions
    in straight line.)
You anoint my head with oil;
my cup overflows.
    (With right thumb, make small
    cross on forehead.)
Only goodness and kindness follow
me all the days of my life;
    (Fold hands, look up.)
And I shall dwell in the house of
the Lord for years to come.
    (Arms and hands raised high,
    look up smiling.)

18

Letter to Parents
Dear Parents,

Include at least part of the 23rd Psalm in your family prayer this week. Our lesson today teaches us we are the sheep of his flock.

Sincerely in Christ,
Teacher _____

Questions
Do we belong to God?

Does God want us to give to others willingly?

Cycle A
First Sunday of Lent

Sorrow For Sins and Avoiding Temptation

Supplies Needed
old calendars (1 per student)

lined slips of paper

pencils

large ashtray and matches

Activity
Begin class by having students X-out forty days of their calendar. Discuss how long forty days is.

Lesson
Jesus went out into the desert to pray and fast [go without food] for forty days and forty nights. [Refer to marked calendars.] Then the tempter [the devil] came and tried to get Jesus to do wrong, but Jesus told Satan [the devil] to go away and angels came and waited on Jesus.

Discuss
How long do we pray each day? (Compare to Jesus praying for forty days.) Any time we want to do something naughty, that is the devil (Satan) testing us. We should say, "In the name of Jesus, Satan go away," as Jesus told Satan to go away.

Explain
Ash Wednesday ashes were put on our forehead. This is a way to say "I am sorry" to God and tell Him "I will try to be a better person."

Liturgy
Students write "I am sorry" on slips of paper. Place slips in a large ashtray on the altar. Join hands, bow heads and say: **Be merciful, O Lord, for we have sinned.**

Teacher burns paper in ashtray.

All sing:
"Joy, Joy, Joy" from "Hi God" record (especially the last verse).

Letter to Parents
Dear Parents,

Lent begins our preparation for Easter. In your family prayer time, include an act of contrition, preferably one a family member makes up so your child understands it.

Sincerely in Christ,
Teacher _____

Questions
When we want to do something wrong, is that Satan testing us?

Should we say, "In Jesus' name, Satan go away"?

If we do wrong, should we say, "I am sorry"?

Does God forgive us when we say, "I am sorry"?

Cycle A
Second Sunday of Lent

We Listen to Jesus

Supplies Needed
large cardboard box

spoons

balloon

paper to tear and crumple

bell

ball

Lesson

Jesus took three of his apostles [friends], Peter, James, and John, up a high mountain and he was transfigured before them. [That means he changed so his face shone like the sun and his clothes became white as light.] A voice from heaven said, "This is my beloved Son, listen to him."

The apostles were afraid and hid their faces. Soon Jesus came and said, "Do not be afraid." And when they looked, Jesus was the same as he always was.

Activity

Play a listening game. Students listen quietly as teacher or helper makes noise behind a box. Students identify what they are hearing.

Example: Clap hands; tap spoons together; ring bell; pop balloon; bounce ball; tear paper; crumple paper; etc. Listen and identify sounds from outside.

Liturgy

Gather around altar. Sit quietly. Close eyes.

Teacher:
In our hearts let us say, "Here I am, Jesus." (Pause.) Now listen to Jesus. (Pause.)

All:
Lord, let your mercy be on us, as we place our trust in you.

Letter to Parents

Dear Parents,

An important part of prayer is listening to God. In your family prayer time, occasionally have a quiet period so each family member can listen to God.

Sincerely in Christ,
Teacher _____

Questions

Did God say Jesus was his Son?
Did God tell us to listen to Jesus?
Can we be still and listen to Jesus in our hearts?

Cycle A
Third Sunday of Lent

To Know Jesus Is the Living Water

Supplies Needed

paper cups (1 per student)
pitcher of water
potting soil
or 1 glass or jar per student
one sweet potato per student
water
flower pots (1 per student)
seeds
toothpicks

Discuss

Water is necessary for life. Water for plants; animals; fish; birds; people.

Activity

Have each student plant seeds or prepare a sweet potato in a jar.

Lesson

One day as Jesus was traveling through a country called Samaria, he grew tired. Jesus sat down to rest by a well known as Jacob's Well. The hour was about noon. When a Samaritan woman came to draw water, Jesus said to her, "Give me a drink." The woman said to Jesus, "You are a Jew. How can you ask me, a Samaritan, for a drink?" [The Jews would have nothing to do with Samaritans.]

(Here pause and discuss prejudice, if your students have been exposed to it. Ask how it feels to be snubbed. Let the students express feelings freely. Then emphasize that Jesus treated all people the same. Jesus loves everyone.)

Jesus said to the woman: "If only you recognized God's gift and who it is that is asking you for a drink, you would have asked him for a drink instead, and he would have given you *living water*."

Jesus was telling the woman, "I am the living water. Water that gives life forever." Jesus is necessary for a good life.

Activity

Each student drinks a glass of water. After each has drunk, have the students then go to the altar and thank God for giving us water.

Liturgy

All together thank God for water. (Then add:)

All:

If today you hear his voice, harden not your hearts.
Jesus come to me, be my living water, so I will always be good. If today you hear his voice, harden not your hearts.

Letter to Parents

Dear Parents,

Today your child is bringing home a seed planted in class (or a sweet potato). Help him/her care for the seed (sweet potato) by watering it properly. Talk about water being necessary for life. Jesus is the living water for our spiritual life.

Sincerely in Christ,
Teacher _____

Questions

Does God give us water to make things grow?
Do animals need water to live?
Do we need water to live?
Is Jesus the living water?
Do we need Jesus?

Cycle A
Fourth Sunday of Lent

We Appreciate Our Gift of Sight

Supplies Needed

blindfolds

Lesson

As Jesus walked along, He saw a man who had been blind from birth. Jesus spat on the ground and made some mud and smeared it on the blind man's eyes. Then Jesus told the man, "Go, wash in the pool of Siloam." So the man went off and washed and came back able to see.

Activity and Liturgy

(Do this in the yard, if possible.) Blindfold each student and have them find their way around. Have them listen to find direction and reach out to feel. Before removing the blindfold, tell each one to imagine they had always been blind and to think how happy they would be when they could see for the first time. Now walk around the yard looking at the beautiful things God has given us. At each, say:

Thank you, God, for the (tree, etc.).
Thank you, God, for letting me see.
The Lord is my shepherd, there is nothing I shall want.

Letter to Parents

Dear Parents,

In your family prayer this week, include, "The Lord is my shepherd, there is nothing I shall want." Also, include a prayer of thanksgiving for the gift of sight.

Sincerely in Christ,
Teacher _____

Questions

Did Jesus cure the blind man so he could see?
Should we thank God for letting us see?

Cycle A
Fifth Sunday of Lent

If We Believe In Jesus, We Will Live Forever

Supplies Needed
large candle
sequins
crucifix
small straight pins
beads
facial tissue

Activity
Decorate the candle. Have each student put something on the candle. When complete, place it on the altar with a small devout procession. Light it and let it burn throughout the class period.

Lesson
When Jesus arrived in a town called Bethany, he found his friend Lazarus had been dead and buried four days. Lazarus' sister, Martha, met Jesus and said, "Lord, if you had been here, my brother would not have died. Even now I am sure God will give you whatever you ask of him."

Jesus said, "Your brother will rise again."

Martha said, "I know he will rise again in the resurrection on the last day."

Jesus said, "I am the resurrection and the life, whoever believes in me though he should die, will come to life, and whoever is alive and believes in me will never die." [Jesus was telling us that if we believe in him, even though we die and leave the other people here on earth, we will still be alive to God in heaven.] Then Jesus had the men roll the stone away from the cave where Lazarus was buried. Jesus looked up and prayed, "Father, I thank you for having heard me. I know you always hear me." Then Jesus called loudly, "Lazarus, come out."

Lazarus came out of the grave.

Stress
Jesus thanked God the Father for his help. In a short while Jesus would also rise from the dead on Easter morning.

Liturgy
On the altar, have a crucifix.

All:
With the Lord there is mercy and fullness of redemption.

(Have veneration of the cross. Let one student hold the crucifix while others kiss it. Wipe it after each with a tissue.)

All:
With the Lord there is mercy and fullness of redemption.

Letter to Parents
Dear Parents,
As a family project, decorate a candle for your Easter candle to burn on the dinner table during Easter week.
                    Sincerely in Christ,
                    Teacher _____

Questions
Should we believe in Jesus?
If we believe in Jesus, will we live with him forever in heaven?

Cycles A-B-C
Palm Sunday

Jesus Dies for Us

Supplies Needed
palm for each student
stapler and staples
crayolas
scissors
egg shapes cut from pastel-
colored construction paper
(see pattern, page 24)

Lesson and Liturgy
The Palm Sunday gospel is the Passion. Go to the church. Walk around the stations of the cross. Discuss each station briefly, then all say: **My God, my God, why have you abandoned me?**

Activity
Make cross of palm by stapling. If time permits, decorate Easter egg-shaped cards for parents. Have cards pre-cut.

Letter to Parents
Dear Parents,

In your family prayer this week, thank Jesus for dying to save us.

No class will be held next week. Have a blessed Easter.

Sincerely in Christ,
Teacher _____

Questions
Did Jesus die for us?
Can we go to heaven because Jesus died for us?

Cycles A-B-C
Second Sunday of Easter

Jesus Is My Lord and My God

Supplies Needed
Banner material, hemmed top and bottom, hem 1 inch deep at the top. Use burlap or drapery sample or other heavy cloth (approximately: 8″ x 11″), 1 per student.
One dowel per student, 1 inch longer than material width.
Yarn, 1 inch longer than dowel, 1 per student.
Pictures of Jesus as an adult, 1 per student.
Felt or construction paper letters, 1 set per student.
Glue.
Matching cards with words: Jesus is my Lord and my God.

Lesson
One day all Jesus' friends were together in a locked room for they were afraid. Jesus had died on the cross and they had heard he had risen from the dead. Suddenly Jesus was there with them. "Peace be to you!" he said. [We say the same thing to each other at Mass.]Then Jesus said, "Go tell other people about me. And whose sins you forgive are forgiven."

Thomas wasn't there. When he returned everyone told him about Jesus' visit. But he said he wouldn't believe unless he could see Jesus and touch his hands and side. Later Jesus came again. Jesus told Thomas to come touch his hands and side. Thomas said, "my Lord and my God."

Liturgy
Gather around altar.

All:
Give thanks to the Lord for he is good, his love is everlasting.

23

EASTER CARD PATTERN
Pre-cut cards. Let students decorate with their own ideas.

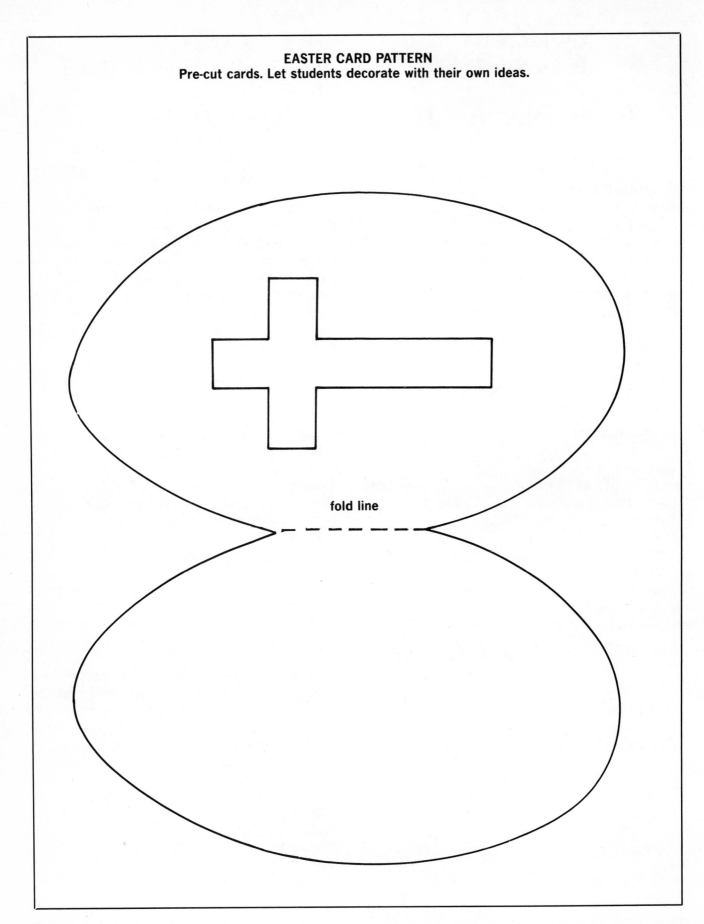

fold line

Sing:
"Thank you, Jesus" to the tune "Amazing Grace."
"Thank you, Jesus, thank you, Jesus, thank you, Jesus, thank you." (repeat)

Wish everyone "The peace of Jesus be with you." Be sure each student says it to every other student in the class. Be sure you do not miss greeting any student.

Activity
Matching cards: Jesus is my Lord and my God (to make and use, see page 2).

Make banners with picture of Jesus and the words: my Lord and my God.

Have students place picture and letters on banner before gluing, so teacher or aide can check for proper sequence.

Letter to Parents
Dear Parents,
Place your child's banner where the family can see it during prayer time. Include in your family prayers this week the greeting of peace from the Mass.
Sincerely in Christ,
Teacher _____

Questions
Is Jesus Lord?
Is Jesus God?
Is Jesus our Lord and God?

Cycle A
Third Sunday of Easter

The Joy of Jesus, Risen

Supplies Needed
Bible
grape juice
paper cups

soft French rolls
napkins

Lesson
Two of Jesus' disciples were walking along the road to a town called Emmaus, when Jesus [who had just risen from the dead] joined them, but they did not recognize [know] Jesus. "What are you talking about?" he asked them.

"Did you not hear about Jesus?" they asked him. Then they told him all about Jesus dying on the cross and being buried. "Then, today, the third day since he died," they said, "some women brought us the most astonishing news. They went early this morning to this tomb [grave] but he was gone. Angels talked to them, and told them Jesus was alive."

Jesus said, "How slow you are." Then he began with Moses and the prophets [people who told of Jesus' coming] and explained the Scripture [Bible] to them [the parts that told about a savior who would come to die for them so they could go to heaven].

It was getting late so they invited Jesus to stay with them. When they sat down to eat Jesus took bread, broke it and gave it to them. Then they recognized [knew] Jesus and Jesus vanished from their sight.

They got up quickly and hurried back to Jerusalem to tell the other disciples.

Activity
Act out the story. Have bread, grape juice and Bible. Use two students as the disciples; one as Jesus; the rest, the disciples in Jerusalem.

Liturgy
Gather around altar. Join hands. (Raise joined hands high for each Jesus is risen, allelulia.)

Leader:
Lord, you will show us the path of life.

All:
Jesus is risen, allelulia.

M Y

L² O² R D

1   2   1   3

A N G

1   1   1

Number under each letter indicates total needed for each student.

Leader:
Lord, You are the path of life.

All:
Jesus is risen, allelulia.

Leader:
Jesus, thank you for coming in Holy Communion.

All:
Jesus is risen, allelulia.

Sing:
Let heaven rejoice and earth be glad,
Let all creation sing.
Let children proclaim through ev'ry land,
"Hosanna to our King."

Letter to Parents
Dear Parents,
Let us be joyful for the Lord is risen. Add a prayer of joy for the risen Lord or a song to your family prayer time this week.
Sincerely in Christ,
Teacher _____

Questions
Did Jesus rise from the dead?
Are we happy Jesus rose from the dead?

Cycle A
Fourth Sunday of Easter

We Know Jesus
We Trust Jesus
He Cares for Us

Supplies Needed
pictures of children and pets
clay
newspaper for tables

Discuss
Our pets: they know us; they trust us; we feed and water them; we care for them—compare this to the shepherd. (Use pictures of children with pets during this discussion.)

Lesson
Jesus told the people the good shepherd [one who cares for sheep] knows all his sheep and his sheep know him. The Good Shepherd comes in through the sheepgate [door] and calls his sheep. The sheep follow the shepherd through the sheepgate. He leads the sheep to find food and water. Then Jesus said a strange thing. He said, "I am the sheepgate. Anyone who comes to me will be safe." We pray to Jesus to care for us as the shepherd cares for his sheep.

Liturgy
Gather around altar. Join hands.

Leader:
Jesus, we know you.

All:
The Lord is my shepherd, there is nothing I shall want.

Leader:
Jesus, we trust you.

All:
The Lord is my shepherd, there is nothing I shall want.

Leader:
Jesus, you care for us.

All:
The Lord is my shepherd, there is nothing I shall want.

Leader:
And you lead us to God, our Father.

All:
Say the Lord's Prayer with gestures. (See page 62.)

Activity
Make clay animals.

Letter to Parents

This week we learned Jesus is the Good Shepherd. During your family prayer time, read the 23rd Psalm.

Sincerely in Christ,
Teacher _____

Questions

Do we know Jesus?
Do we trust Jesus?
Does Jesus care for us?

Cycle A
Fifth Sunday of Easter

Jesus Is the Way to God Our Father

Supplies Needed

maze (1 per student,
see pattern this page)
pencils

Lesson

Last week we heard that Jesus said he was the sheepgate. Another time Jesus said, "I am the way, the truth and the life. No one comes to the Father except through me."

The sheep have to go through the sheepgate to get food and water. We have to go through Jesus to get to God the Father in heaven. [Do you know the way to school? Or work? Do you know the way home today? Could you find the way home if no one came to pick you up? How would you find your way? What would you ask people? If we want to get someplace new, we ask, "What way do I go?"

To get to God the Father, Jesus said, "I am the way." We trust Jesus to lead us to God our Father.

Liturgy

Gather around altar.

All:

Lord, let your mercy be on us, as we place our trust in you. "Jesus," you said, "I am the way, the truth and the life, please lead me to God our Father."

Say the Lord's Prayer with gestures. (See page 62.)

Sing:

Tune: "Joy, Joy, Joy
I've got the Father, Son and Holy Spirit, deep in my heart," etc.

Activity

Give each student a maze to work. (See this page.)

Letter to Parents

Dear Parents,

Include the Lord's Prayer in your family prayers this week. Attached is a copy of the prayer with the gestures we use in class. This makes the prayer more meaningful to your child. Encourage him/her to say the Lord's Prayer in his/her night prayers. Use the gestures at this time also.

Sincerely in Christ,
Teacher _____

Questions

Did Jesus say, "I am the Way"?
Is Jesus the Way to God our Father?
Will Jesus lead us to God our Father?

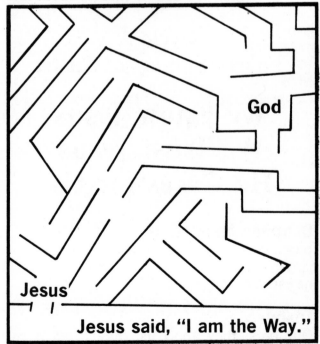

Jesus said, "I am the Way."

Find the way to God, start with Jesus.

Cycle A
Sixth Sunday of Easter

The Holy Spirit Helps Us Jesus Is Preparing a Place for Us in Heaven

Supplies Needed
balloons
marking pens (permanent ink)
string
tank of helium (and a father to operate it)
postcards (see Activity for preparation)

Lesson
Jesus said, "If you love me, be good. I will send the Holy Spirit to help you to be good. I am going to heaven to be with my father, and prepare a place for you."

Discuss
Sometimes it is hard to be good. It is nice to know we have the Holy Spirit to help us.

Liturgy
Gather around altar. Join hands.

Leader:
Come, Holy Spirit.

All:
Let all the earth cry out with joy.

Leader:
Help us to be good.

All:
Let all the earth cry out with joy.

Leader:
Lead us to Jesus and God, our Father.

All:
Let all the earth cry out with joy.

Say:
Lord's Prayer (with gestures).

Sing:
(Tune: "Joy, Joy, Joy") "I've got the Father, Son and Holy Spirit, deep in my heart," etc.

Discuss
Jesus also said, "I am going to heaven to be with my father, and *prepare a place for you.*" Just think, Jesus is preparing a special place for each of us. Let us close our eyes and think about that for a minute. (Give the students time to meditate on this thought, but do not tax their ability to be still too long. Ask the students to tell how they feel about knowing Jesus is preparing a place especially for them. After each has told how he or she feels, repeat the psalm: Let All the Earth Cry Out with Joy. All join hands, raise them high and shout the psalm.)

Activity
With marking pens, print JOY on the balloons. Fill them with helium; tie strings with postcards to each balloon. When all prepared, take into the school yard and release.

Cards: On one side, have typed:

```
Place Found_____
When Found_____
By Whom_____
The joy of the Lord be with you. Please mail
this card back to us. Thank you.
```

On the other side, have different students' return addresses.

Letter to Parents
Dear Parents,
Today we learned Jesus promised to send the Holy Spirit to help us. Also, Jesus is preparing a special place for us in heaven. Include in your family prayers a request for the Holy Spirit to guide and strengthen you.

Add a prayer of thanks to Jesus for preparing a special place for us.

Sincerely in Christ,
Teacher _____

Questions
Did Jesus promise to send the Holy Spirit?
Will the Holy Spirit help us to be good?
Is Jesus preparing a place for us in heaven?

Cycle A
Seventh Sunday of Easter

Jesus Prays:
We Pray with Jesus

Note to Teacher: Have class sit around altar on chairs. Today's lesson is all prayer.

Discuss
Many times in our lessons we have heard that Jesus went off by himself to pray to God, his Father. Today we have a prayer Jesus said a short time before he was to die to save us. We are going to join Jesus in that prayer today.

(Have the students put their feet flat on the floor. Let hands rest in lap in an open prayer position. All close eyes. Have an aide read each section of the prayer, then pause while the teacher explains. Tell the students the aide will read Jesus' words. Two voices are necessary for this lesson.)

Read slowly and distinctly:
Reader:
Jesus looked up to heaven and said: "Father, the hour has come!"

Teacher:
Jesus knew it was time for him to die for our sins.

All:
I believe that I shall see the good things of the Lord in the land of the living.

Reader:
Give glory to your son that your son may give glory to you.

Teacher:
After Jesus died he would rise in glory. This would be Jesus' glory and prove God's glory.

All:
I believe that I shall see the good things of the Lord in the land of the living.

Reader:
You have given me authority over all mankind, that I may bestow eternal life on those you gave me.

Teacher:
Those who love and follow Jesus will one day live in heaven with him.

All:
I believe that I shall see the good things of the Lord in the land of the living.

Reader:
Eternal life is this: to know you, the only true God, and Him whom you have sent, Jesus Christ.

Teacher:
Eternal life is heaven where we will know God the Father and Jesus also.

All:
I believe that I shall see the good things of the Lord in the land of the living.

Reader:
I have given you glory on earth by finishing the work you gave me to do.

Teacher:
We also give glory to God by doing all the things we are supposed to do.

All:
I believe that I shall see the good things of the Lord in the land of the living.

Reader:
I have made your name known to those you gave me.

Teacher:
Jesus told us all about God, our Father; otherwise we would not know him at all.

All:
I believe that I shall see the good things of the Lord in the land of the living.

Reader:
These men have kept our word.

Teacher:
The apostles lived as God wanted them to live. We can do the same.

All:
I believe that I shall see the good things of the Lord in the land of the living.

Reader:
I entrusted to them the message you trusted to me.

Teacher:
Jesus trusted the apostles to tell others about God. Jesus trusts us to tell people about God.

All:
I believe that I shall see the good things of the Lord in the land of the living.

Reader:
They have known that in truth I came from you. They have believed it was you who sent me.

Teacher:
The apostles believed that God sent Jesus into the world. We believe that God sent Jesus into the world.

All:
I believe that I shall see the good things of the Lord in the land of the living.

Reader:
I am in the world no more, but these are in the world as I come to you.

Teacher:
Jesus was soon to die and go back to his Father. He would leave behind on earth all the people who believed in him and loved him.

All:
I believe that I shall see the good things of the Lord in the land of the living.

Activity
Let us all stand up and stretch as high as we can. (Have a good stretch.) Now let us touch our toes. (Repeat as many times as you feel necessary for your class.)

Now reaching toward heaven, sing "Praise God" to the tune: "Amazing Grace." Repeat the phrase "Praise God" throughout song.

Letter to Parents
We spent our class period in prayer. Jesus often spent time praying and today we joined him in prayer. In your family prayer, often include a few minutes in quiet listening to God.

Sincerely in Christ,
Teacher _____

Questions
Did Jesus pray?
Can we pray with Jesus?

Cycles A-B-C
Pentecost Sunday

The Holy Spirit Dwells in Us and Strengthens Us

Supplies Needed

1 heart and rectangle per student (see pattern page 33)	glue
	pens

Lesson

After Jesus was crucified, his disciples [followers] were afraid so they spent most of their time in a locked room. One evening Jesus came to them and said, "Peace be with you." He showed them his hands and side. The disciples rejoiced [were happy] to see Jesus. Again Jesus said, "Peace be with you." Then Jesus said, "Receive the Holy Spirit. If you forgive men's sins, they are forgiven them."

Discuss

The Holy Spirit is God, just as Jesus is God and God the Father is God. The Holy Spirit lives in us. The Holy Spirit gives us the strength to be good [helps us to be good]. It is by the Holy Spirit that our sins are forgiven.

Sing:

Tune: "Joy, Joy, Joy"
I've got the Father, Son and Holy Spirit deep in my heart, deep in my heart, deep in my heart. I've got the Father, Son and Holy Spirit deep in my heart, deep in my heart to stay.

Liturgy

Gather around altar. Repeat song.

All:

Give thanks to the Lord for he is good, his love is everlasting.
(Pause and think about how good the Lord is.)

All:

Give thanks to the Lord for he is good, his love is everlasting.

Activity

Make heart with door in it. When door opens, it reads: Come, Holy Spirit. (See patterns, page 33.)

Letter to Parents

Dear Parents,
The Holy Spirit dwells within us and strengthens us. In your family prayer time this week, include "Come Holy Spirit, fill us with your love."

Sincerely in Christ,
Teacher _____

Questions

Does the Holy Spirit live in us?
Does the Holy Spirit help us to be good?

Cycles A-B-C
Trinity Sunday

Jesus Has Chosen Us For His Own

Supplies Needed

1 sheet poster board
seals of Jesus
scissors
marking pen
red hearts (2 per student)
cut from construction paper
9" × 12" sheet construction paper (1 per student); on it have printed: Let Jesus into your heart.

Lesson

Jesus told his disciples to go and make disciples [followers] of all the nations [countries] of the world. "Baptize them in the name of the Father and of the Son and of the Holy Spirit. Teach them to do all things I have commanded you."

Discuss

Can you tell me what Jesus wanted the disciples to teach?
Were they to teach that God loves everyone?
Were they to teach that Jesus died for us?
Were they to teach the people to love everyone?
Are you a disciple of Jesus?
Have you got the Father, Son and Holy Spirit in you?

Pattern for Holy Spirit Heart

1. Cut 1 rectangle of white construction paper, per student.
2. Glue outer edge only.
3. Pre-print some for students who cannot print own.
4. One heart cut of red construction paper per student.
5. Cut along dotted lines in center of heart.

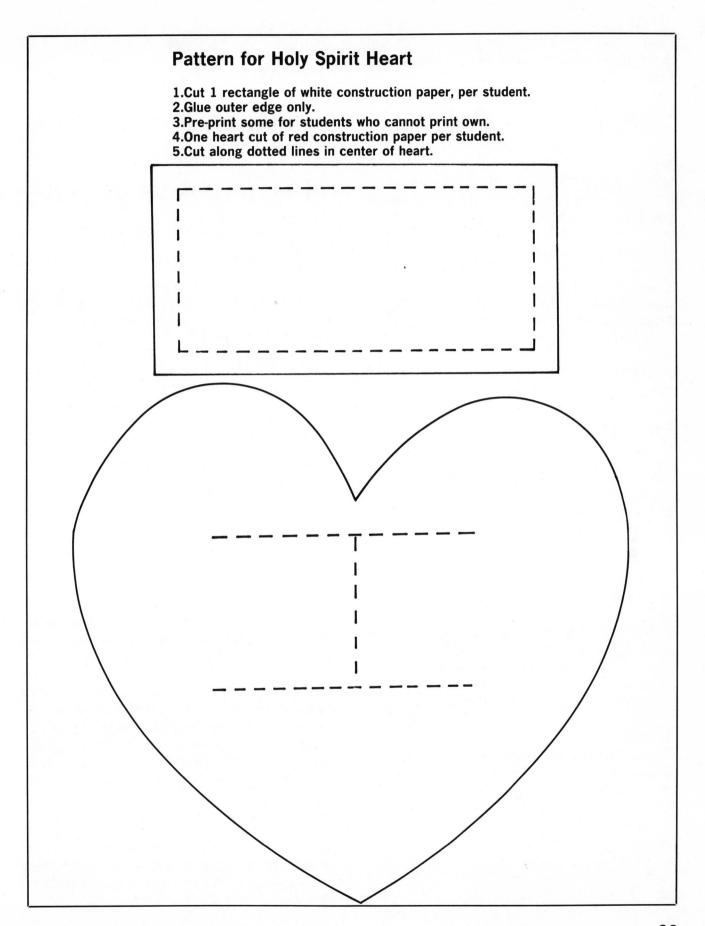

33

Let us sing (tune: "Joy, Joy, Joy"): I've got the Father, Son and Holy Spirit, deep in my heart, etc.

Liturgy
Gather around altar. Join hands.

All:
Happy the people the Lord has chosen to be his own. Jesus, we are your disciples. Jesus, you have chosen us to be your own. Thank you, Jesus. Happy the people the Lord has chosen to be his own.

Sing:
tune: "Amazing Grace."
Thank you, Jesus, thank you, Jesus,
Thank you Jesus, thank you. (Repeat.)

Activity
Make poster. Each student cuts out a heart; puts a seal of Jesus on it and glues it to the poster board on which is printed WE HAVE JESUS IN OUR HEARTS. Each student writes his/her name under his or her heart. On a 9" × 12" sheet of construction paper, have students glue a heart with Jesus on it and add the words: LET JESUS INTO YOUR HEART. Take this home for the family.

Letter to Parents
Dear Parents,
   Jesus has chosen us for his own. In your family prayers, sing to the tune "Amazing Grace." Repeat the phrase "Thank you, Jesus" three times, then the words "thank you" once. Repeat between a second time.
                          Sincerely in Christ,
                          Teacher ———————

Questions
Does God love everyone?
Does God want everyone to love him?
Is Jesus in our hearts?
Do we belong to Jesus?
Did Jesus choose us?

Cycle A
Twenty-third Sunday of Year

Students, Helpers and Teacher Become Acquainted
We Must Forgive Those Who Wrong Us
Jesus Is With Us When We Pray Together

Supplies Needed
name tags (see pattern, page 36)
Jesus stickers
altar cloth
2 candles
Bible
Bible stand
candle holders
Have name tags ready. As students arrive, each should find own tag if possible. Read tag to students who cannot read. Give each student a sticker of Jesus to place on name tag.

Activity
Today is the first class after summer vacation. Take time for new students to get acquainted with classmates and teachers. Talk about the highlights of their summer vacations. When all are at ease, begin the lesson.

Lesson
One day Jesus was teaching his friends and he told them: "If someone does something wrong to you, tell him nicely that what he has done is wrong. Try to make him understand that you forgive him and want to be friends."

That is not an easy thing Jesus told us to do. But if we remember that we want others to forgive us if we do wrong and say a prayer to Jesus to help us forgive others, it will be easier. [Talk about Sunday's responsorial psalm here: "If today you hear his voice, harden not your hearts."]

We should ask others to pray with us for Jesus also said that if two or more people prayed together, he was with them.

Liturgy

Gather around altar. Ask one student to put the altar cloth on the altar. Have another student place the Bible stand in the center of the altar. Have two students place candles on each side of the Bible stand. Holding the Bible reverently, explain: This book is called the Bible. The Bible is God's book for it is his word. Because it is God's word, we like to read it and take good care of it. [Open Bible to Matthew 18:15–20.]

Here is where I found Jesus' story I told you today. Ask another student to place the Bible on the stand in an open position. Remind students: Jesus said, "When two or more people pray together I am with them." Join hands and pray: Thank you, Jesus, for being with us now. Thank you for bringing us all together for our class. [Ask students if they have anything to thank Jesus for; then add:] Jesus, I forgive everyone who has done anything wrong to me. If today you hear his voice, harden not your hearts.

[Have students help put away altar supplies. Let the students set up the altar before class in the future.]

Letter to Parents

Dear Parents,

Today's lesson was about forgiving others and praying together. Jesus said, "Where two or three are gathered in my name, there am I in their midst."

Take a few minutes each day this week to pray together as a family unit. Remind everyone before prayer that when you pray together Jesus is with you.

Sincerely in Christ,
Teacher _____

Questions

If someone does something wrong to us, what should we do? (Forgive them.)

or

If someone does something wrong to us, should we forgive them?

Where did Jesus say he would be when we pray together? (With us.)

Cycle A
Twenty-fourth Sunday of Year

God Will Forgive Us As We Forgive We Must Forgive Others Many Times

Supplies Needed

lined paper (1 sheet per student)
pencils

Lesson

Last week we talked about Jesus telling his friends to forgive anyone who does them wrong. One day Peter asked Jesus, "How many times must I forgive someone who does me wrong? Seven times?" [Can anyone show me how many seven times is?] Jesus answered Peter and said, "Not seven times but seventy times seven."

[Stop here and have students do the Activity. When finished, go on with the parable.]

Activity

Have students mark paper 490 times with ┼┼┼┼. (This may seem boring to teachers and helpers, but the students are fascinated by the number of marks on their paper.) *Stress:* This is how often we must forgive each person who offends us. Have students

NAME TAG PATTERN

Cut 2 per student.
Punch holes at X's.
With yarn, fasten 2 hearts together allowing enough room for student to wear scapular fashion. (See Fig. 1.)

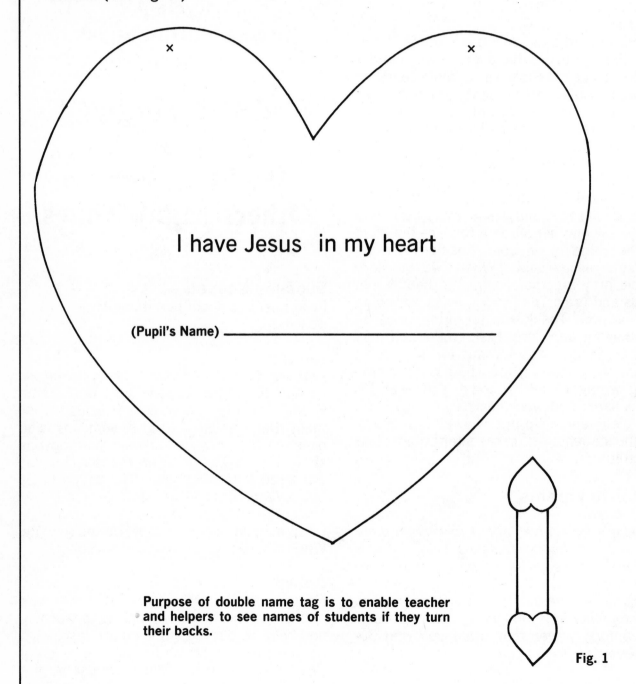

×   ×

I have Jesus in my heart

(Pupil's Name) _____

Purpose of double name tag is to enable teacher and helpers to see names of students if they turn their backs.

Fig. 1

take paper home to hang in room as a reminder.

Lesson
After Jesus answered Peter he told them a story about a king who had a servant that owed him some money. The king demanded his servant to pay what he owed or be punished. The servant begged the king to give him more time and he would pay what he owed. The king felt sorry for the man and gave him more time to pay.

The man went home and on his way he met a fellow worker who owed him some money, but not nearly as much as the first man owed the king.

The first man demanded his fellow worker to pay what he owed. His fellow worker begged for more time, promising to pay what he owed. But the first man said, "No" and had his fellow worker punished for not paying his debt [what he owed].

When the king heard what had happened he said to the first man, "You worthless person. I forgave you, you should have forgiven your fellow worker. Just for that I will punish you."

Then Jesus said, "God, my heavenly father, will forgive you the same way you forgive others."

Discuss
Meaning of God forgiving us as we forgive others.

Liturgy
Gather around altar.

Explain: Today's psalm means the same as our discussion. God will forgive us as we forgive others. Explain: Phrase from the Lord's Prayer, "and forgive us our trespasses as we forgive those who trespass against us."

Join hands.

All:
The Lord is kind and merciful; slow to anger, and rich in compassion. Add the Lord's Prayer with gestures. See page 62.

Letter to Parents
Dear Parents,
Again this week our theme is forgiveness. God forgives us the same way we forgive others. We ask for this kind of forgiveness in the Lord's Prayer.
This week, continue to pray together as a family unit saying the Our Father.
Sincerely in Christ,
Teacher _____

Questions
How many times must we forgive each person who hurts us in any way? (The answer you want should indicate the students know they must always forgive others.)

If we forgive others, will God forgive us?

If we do not forgive others, will God forgive us?

Cycle A
Twenty-fifth Sunday of Year

God Wants Us to Do Our Duty, Cheerfully

Supplies Needed
seedless grapes
crayolas
long strip of brown wrapping paper
thumb tacks

Note to Teacher
Begin class by giving each student a small bunch of seedless grapes to eat.

Lesson
One day Jesus told this parable [story] to his disciples[followers]. There was a man who

owned a vineyard [a grape farm]. He hired some men early one morning to work in his vineyard. They agreed to what they would be paid at the end of the day. Several times later that day the man went out and hired more workers; some he hired quite late in the afternoon. At the end of the day he paid all the workers the same amount. The men who had worked all day grumbled because they thought they should have more. But the man said, "You should not be jealous for I paid you what we agreed on."

Jesus told the parable to explain about heaven. If we live and do as God wants us to do, when we die we will go to heaven, no matter how old we are. An old man or a small child can both go to heaven if they live as God wants them to live.

Liturgy
Gather around altar. Say or sing the Lord's Prayer with gestures. Add: The Lord is near to all who call on him.

Activity
Discuss with the students: What do you think God wants you to do? Draw out ideas like: pray; obey; do chores; study; have fun; be cheerful, etc. Have students make a mural of children doing the things discussed. Use a strip of brown wrapping paper long enough so each student has enough room to work. Pin up in the classroom when finished.

Letter to Parents
Dear Parents,

Our psalm this week is: The Lord Is Near to All Who Call on Him. Continue to pray as a family unit. Say the Lord's Prayer, then ask the children if they have something special to say to God. Encourage them to talk to God as a friend.

Sincerely in Christ,
Teacher _____

Questions
Does God want us to be good?
Does God want us to do our chores?
Should we do our chores cheerfully?

Cycle A
Twenty-sixth Sunday of Year

Obedience Is Best When It Is Prompt and Cheerful

Supplies Needed
mural from last lesson
"I Obey My Parents" certificates
(see page 39)

Discuss
Mural from last week.

Lesson
One day Jesus told the leaders of the people this story. A man had two sons. He asked the first son to go work in the vineyard [the grape farm]. The son said, "Yes," to his father, but went off and did something else instead.

The man asked his second son to go work in the vineyard. The son said, "No," to his father. Later he was sorry he had said "No" and he went to the vineyard to work. Jesus asked the leaders of the people which boy did what the father wanted. They said, "The second son." When our parents ask us to do something, we should say "yes" like the first son and do what our parents ask like the second son.

Activity
Discuss obedience: If Mother or Father tells us to do something, do we say "yes" or "no"? Do we do what our parents ask with a smile on our face? Role-play obeying: Select a Mother, Father and child. Let students make up their own scene. Sing (tune: "Mulberry Bush"): "This is the way we [name chores students do]." "I obey my parents

club." Have students add their name to the certificate.

Liturgy

Gather around the altar. Join hands.

All:

Dear Jesus, help me to always obey my parents, teachers and anyone who cares for me. When I am asked to do something, I will say "yes" and do it cheerfully. Remember your mercies, O Lord.

Letter to Parents

Dear Parents,

Today our theme was obedience. In your prayer this week, encourage the children to add: "Jesus, help me to always obey cheerfully."

Sincerely in Christ,
Teacher _____

Questions

When our parents ask us to do something, do we say "yes" or "no"?
Do we obey cheerfully?
Do we obey promptly?

Certificate

_____

(student's name)

belongs to "I Obey My Parents Club"

Cycle A
Twenty-seventh Sunday of Year

We Are God's People

Supplies Needed
paper plates with 2 holes punched near edge for hanging, and printed with: We are God's vineyard (1 per student)
small pieces of yarn (1 per student)
glue or library paste
holy cards or pictures of Jesus on the cross
purple crayolas for grapes
green crayolas for leaves

Lesson
(Explain: A parable is a story with a hidden meaning in it. Jesus told parables all the time.)

One day Jesus told the leaders of the people this parable. A man owned a vineyard [grape farm]. He hired some men to take care of it while he went on a trip. When vintage time arrived [that is the time when the grapes are picked], the man sent some of his servants [workers] to collect his share for him. The men who were taking care of the vineyard beat the servants up and even killed one.

The owner of the vineyard sent a larger number of servants the second time, but the men taking care of the vineyard did the same to these servants.

The owner of the vineyard then sent his son for he thought they would not harm his son, but they killed his son.

The hidden meaning is this: the grapes were like the people the leaders were supposed to care for. The owner of the vineyard was God who sent his Son. Jesus was telling the leaders of the people that he knew they were planning to put him to death.

Activity
Mount pictures of Jesus on the cross on paper plates. Have students decorate edge of plate by drawing pictures of grapes. Each plate should have the words "We are God's vineyard" printed at the bottom. Punch 2 holes at top. Run yarn through the holes and tie for a hanger. Pictures can be found on sympathy cards, or purchase enough holy cards for your class.

Liturgy
Gather around altar. Join hands.

All:
The vineyard of the Lord is the house of Israel.
(God's chosen people.)

We are God's vineyard. We are his people.

Jesus, we thank you for coming to us and dying for us.

Letter to Parents
Dear Parents,
Have your child explain the plate he/she decorated in class. At family prayer time this week, say, "Jesus, thank you for dying for us. Thank you, for making us your people."
Sincerely in Christ,
Teacher _____

Questions (Ask these as the students do the Activity.)
Who is God's Son?
Are we God's people?
Does God care for us?
Does God love us?
Does Jesus love us?

Cycle A
Twenty-eighth Sunday of Year

God Invites Us All to Heaven

Supplies Needed
party hats
paper cups
juice
favors
paper napkins
cookies

Activity
When students arrive, have a table set for a party. Have party hats, favors, cookies and juice. Ask each student if he/she would like to come to your party. Enjoy yourselves.

Lesson
Jesus told another parable [story] about a king who prepared a wedding feast [a big party] for his son. He sent his servants [men who worked for him] out to tell the people who were invited to "Come, the feast is ready." But they would not come. So again he sent more servants to tell the people to "Come, the feast is ready." But they had all kinds of reasons why they did not want to come to the wedding feast. Some even got mad and killed the servants. The king, when he heard what happened, sent his army against the people. Then he sent his servants out into the streets to ask everyone they met to come to the wedding feast. The wedding feast was filled with guests.

The hidden meaning is this: the king is God. The wedding feast is heaven. God sent Jesus for his chosen people, but they would not accept Jesus and learn how to get to heaven. So God invited everyone to hear about Jesus and learn how to get to heaven. The servants of the king are your priests and teachers who tell you about Jesus, God and heaven.

Liturgy
Explain: We all want to go to heaven and live forever with God. Today in our prayer we call heaven "The House of the Lord."

Gather around the altar; join hands.

All:
I shall live in the house of the Lord all the days of my life.

Sing:
(tune: "Three Blind Mice." Do as a round if possible. Make your liturgy joyful.)

God says to all
God says to all
Come to heaven
Come to heaven
Go out and tell everyone
Come and live with my son
We're inviting everyone
Come to heaven

Letter to Parents
Dear Parents,

God, our Father, has made heaven a special place for us. This week in your family prayer, include the Lord's Prayer and the psalm: I Shall Live in the House of the Lord All the Days of My Life.

Sincerely in Christ,
Teacher _____

Questions
Does God invite us to heaven?
Will we live there with Jesus?

Cycle A
Twenty-ninth Sunday of Year

Praise and Thank God for All His Gifts, Especially Nature

Lesson

The pharisees [leaders of the people] wanted to trick Jesus into saying something wrong. They asked Jesus if it was all right with God for them to pay taxes to Caesar [the ruler of the people]. Jesus knew they were trying to trick him. He said to them, "Let me see the money you use to pay the tax." The pharisees gave Jesus a coin. [A penny is a coin.] Jesus said, "Whose picture is on this coin?" They said, "Caesar's." Jesus told them, "Give to Caeser the things that are Caesar's and give to God the things that are God's." Jesus is telling us to pay what we must, also give God what is his.

[Here encourage the students to tell what they should give to God, or tell them if they are unable to respond. Love; thanks; all we do, say and think.]

Liturgy

Gather around altar. With arms raised heavenward, say: Give the Lord glory and honor.

Add a morning offering using gestures:

Dear Father in heaven (arms raised heavenward)
We give you this day (arms and hands stretched forward as though handing something to someone)
All we think (point to head)
And do (hands open and out from sides)
And say. (point to mouth)
Amen. (fold hands)

Sing:

"Praise God" the tune "Amazing Grace." Repeat words "Praise God" throughout entire tune.

Activity

Take a nature walk. Have students point out things they see that God made. As each item is pointed out, have the students say, "Thank you, God." You may even want to sing "Praise God" as you are walking.

Letter to Parents

Dear Parents,
Today we learned a morning offering to do with gestures so it is more meaningful to your child. Begin your day saying it together. (Add prayer here.)
We went on a nature walk praising and thanking God for all his creation. Whenever you are out of doors with your child, call his/her attention to God's beautiful creation and be sure to praise and thank him.
Sincerely in Christ,
Teacher _____

Questions

What can we give God?
Shall we give him thanks?
Shall we give him praise?
Shall we give him our love?

Cycle A
Thirtieth Sunday of Year

We Love God First We Love Everyone

Supplies Needed

styrofoam egg cartons (various colors)
pipe cleaners
glue
green construction paper leaves
(see pattern, page 43)
red construction paper hearts
(see pattern, page 43)
pins

Note to Teacher

Begin class by giving each student a red construction paper heart that says, "I Love God," to pin on. Be sure to read it to each student who cannot read.

Lesson

Once again the Pharisees [leaders of the people] tried to trick Jesus into saying something wrong. They asked Jesus, "What is the greatest commandment?" [law or rule we live by]. Jesus said, "You must love the Lord your God with all your heart [place hand on heart] and mind [point to head] and soul [every bit of you]. That is the first and greatest commandment and the second commandment is: You must love your neighbor [everyone] as yourself."

Discuss

If we love God, how do we show it? (Encourage students to tell you the answer.) By being good. Doing all we should do. Praying and thanking God for loving us. By always being nice to others. (If they cannot answer, rephrase the questions to include the answer.)

Activity

Make artificial flowers. Take to church and place on side altar in a vase.

Liturgy

Do in church after placing flowers on altar. Encourage students to make up prayers telling God they love him, praise him and thank him. End with all saying: **I love you, Lord, my strength.**

Letter to Parents

Dear Parents,

Today we learned about the two greatest commandments. Love God with your whole heart and mind and soul and love your neighbor as yourself. Continue your family prayer with the morning offering.

Sincerely in Christ,
Teacher _____

Questions

Do we show God our love by being good?
Do we love God first before everything and everyone else?
Do we love everyone?

To Make Flowers: Use colored styrofoam egg cartons. Cut individual cups into tulip shapes (Fig. 1). Use colored pipe cleaners for stems. Make a small loop at one end of pipe cleaner (Fig. 2). Loop prevents pipe cleaner from coming all the way through egg cup.

Force straight end down through center of egg cup (Fig. 3).
Glue construction paper leaf to stem (Fig. 4). See leaf pattern.

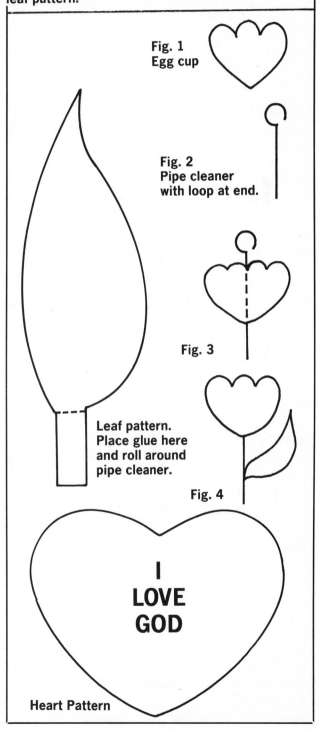

Fig. 1
Egg cup

Fig. 2
Pipe cleaner with loop at end.

Fig. 3

Leaf pattern. Place glue here and roll around pipe cleaner.

Fig. 4

I LOVE GOD

Heart Pattern

Cycle A
Thirty-first Sunday of Year

To Be Great One Must Serve Others

Supplies Needed
paper napkins
juice
graham crackers
paper cups
can opener

Activity
Have a treat today of graham crackers and juice. Have the students share the work of preparing the treat. Be sure each student has something to do according to his/her abilities. (You can make several simple tasks for the students: count out napkins; pass out napkins; count out paper cups; divide graham crackers; pour juice and serve.)

Discuss
The joy of doing your share. How nice it is to serve others. Let students tell how they felt while serving others.

Lesson
Jesus told his disciples [followers] that the greatest among them must be a servant to the others. [A servant is one who serves or waits on others, as each of you did today.] Jesus said that anyone who is willing to serve others will one day be blessed by God.

Liturgy
Gather around altar.

All:
In you, O Lord, I have found my peace. Say the following prayer (or sing to the tune of "Thank You, Lord," from "Hi God"):

Thank you, Lord, for your peace.

Thank you, Lord, for giving us [here mention the feelings the students spoke of while discussing serving others.]

End with an exchange of a greeting of peace.

Letter to Parents
Dear Parents,
The theme of today's lesson was "The greatest among you will be the one who serves the rest." This week, have your child serve at meal time to the fullest of his/her ability. Encourage him/her to discuss his/her feelings in being able to serve others.
Sincerely in Christ,
Teacher _____

Questions
Do we want to be great in God's eyes?
Should we serve (help) others?

Cycle A
Thirty-second Sunday of Year

We Are Ready for God When We Are Good We Must Always Be Good

Supplies Needed
pyrex cup
cooking oil
string soaked in oil
matches
weight (small bolt or washer)

Activity
Make an oil-burning candle.

To make: Have a piece of string that you have soaked until saturated in cooking oil. Drain on a paper towel. Fill a pyrex cup ½ full of cooking oil. Tie a weight on one end of string and place in center of cup for wick. Light string. Burns like a candle.

Discuss: When Jesus lived on earth, no one had electric lights so they made their lights using oil. To walk at night, they did not have flashlights so they carried oil-burning lamps.

Lesson
One day Jesus told a parable [story] about heaven. Once ten virgins [ten good unmarried women] took their lamps and went to meet the bride and groom. Five wise virgins took oil for their lamps, but five foolish virgins did not take oil for their lamps. The groom and bride were late so the ten virgins fell asleep. At midnight someone awoke them shouting "The groom and bride are coming. Go meet them." The five wise virgins lit their lamps, but the five foolish could not light theirs for they had not brought extra oil. They asked the wise virgins to give them oil, but they said, "No, if we do we will all run out of oil. Go buy yourselves some oil." While the five foolish were buying oil, the groom and bride arrived and went on to their house with the five wise virgins. When the five foolish virgins finally got oil for their lamps, the doors were all locked, and they could not get in. Jesus told the people to be ready like the five wise virgins so when God comes we can go meet him. That is the hidden meaning of this story Jesus told.

Discuss
We are ready for God when we are good. We must always be good.

Liturgy
Discuss: "thirsting." "We thirst for something" means we want it very much.

All:
My soul is thirsting for you, O Lord, my God. Jesus, help me to be good so I will be ready when you come. Come, Lord Jesus, come. My soul is thirsting for you, O Lord, my God.

Letter to Parents
Dear Parents,
Make an "uncandle" to burn during family prayer. (Instructions attached.)

Our prayer today was: Jesus, Help Me to Be Good So I Will Be Ready When You Come. Come, Lord Jesus, Come.
Sincerely in Christ,
Teacher _____

Questions
Should we always be ready for God?
Are we ready when we are good?

Cycle A
Thirty-third Sunday of Year

We Must Use the Abilities God Gave Us

Lesson
One day Jesus told the parable [story] of a man who was going on a trip. He called his servants [those who worked for him] and gave them his money to take care of for him. To one man he gave 5,000 silver pieces; to another he gave two and to another he gave one, according to his ability. When the man came home from his trip he called his servants to see how well they had taken care of his money. The servant who had 5,000 pieces of silver came and said, "See, you gave me 5,000 pieces of silver and I have made 5,000 more."

Discuss
Do you think that made the man happy? God is like the man going on a trip. We are like the servants. God gives each of us abilities (things we can do well). God wants us to use our abilities and do even better. Tell me something you can do well. (Let each pupil talk about his/her abilities. Let the students demonstrate if possible. Give praise and encouragement.)

Activity

Sing: "I am Special" with gestures.

I Am Special (thumbs at armpits, palms open)
I Am Special (thumbs at armpits, palms open)
If You Look You Will See (hands at forehead, shading eyes looking all directions)
Someone Very Special (thumbs at armpits, palms open)
Someone Very Special (thumbs at armpits, palms open)
Yes, It's Me, Yes, It's Me (nod "Yes," point to self)

Liturgy

Gather around altar. Explain that "fear" used in the psalm means "love."

All:

Happy are those who fear the Lord.
Have each student say in turn: Thank You, Lord, for my ability to [student states ability discussed in the lesson].

After each, all respond with: Happy are those who fear the Lord.

Letter to Parents

Dear Parents,
*   Today our lesson was on using the abilities God gave each of us. Encourage your child to use his/her abilities to their fullest. In your family prayer, include: Thank You, Lord, for My Ability to [each person states own ability]. Remember our greatest ability is to love one another.*

Sincerely in Christ,
Teacher _____

Questions

Did God give each of us abilities? (Something we do best?)
Should we use our abilities for others?

We Should See Jesus in Others

Supplies Needed

colored construction paper
glue
crayolas
scissors
pens
pictures from greeting cards

Lesson

One day Jesus will come in glory like a great king to judge everyone. To the good he will say, "Come to me for I was hungry and you gave me food. I was thirsty and you gave me a drink. I was a stranger and you made me welcome. I was naked and you gave me clothes. I was sick and you visited me. I was in prison and you came to see me."

Then the good will say, "When did we see you hungry and give you food, or thirsty and give you a drink? When did we see you a stranger and make you welcome? Or naked and give you clothes? When were you sick or in prison and we visited you?"

Then Jesus will say, "Whenever you did it to the least of my brothers you did it to me."

Explain

Everyone is Jesus' brother so whenever we do good to anyone we do it to Jesus.

Discuss

If your parish has a Thanksgiving food and clothing drive, it is one way to feed the hungry and clothe the naked (poor). Maybe some of your students have participated in a "walk for the poor" or a "jog-a-thon for the poor'' or similar activity; have them tell about it. Discuss other local ways of helping the poor. Ask if anyone knows someone who is sick.

Liturgy
Gather around altar. Join hands.

All:
The Lord is my shepherd, there is nothing I shall want. Jesus, help us to see you in others.
Let there be enough food and clothes for the poor. Take care of all the sick and lonely especially [here name any sick people the students know]. The Lord is my shepherd, there is nothing I shall want.

Activity
Make a greeting card for a sick friend. (If they don't know anyone who is ill, make greeting cards for the lonely aged in a nearby nursing home.) Or plan ahead with a nursing home staff to bring your class for a visit to the aged.

Greeting cards: Let students select supplies and use their own creative ability.

Letter to Parents
Dear Parents,
Sunday's gospel should make us aware of the poor, the sick and the lonely. Encourage your child to participate in local activities to aid the poor, sick and lonely. In your family prayer, include prayers for these people.
Sincerely in Christ,
Teacher _____
N.B. Please send a rolling pin to class with your child next week.

Questions
Is everyone Jesus' brother?
Should we do good for others?
If we do good for others, are we doing good for Jesus?

Note to Teacher
Next week go to the First Sunday of Advent—Cycle B (page 48).

CYCLE B

Cycle B
First Sunday of Advent

Always Be Prepared to Meet Jesus

Supplies Needed
rolling pins (students bring own)
1 large grocery sack per student
(Have students name on the outside of sack.)
spatula
round toothpicks
oil cloth or other protective
covering for table top
cookie cutters (religious Christmas shapes)
patterns (see page 49)
baker's clay (recipe below)
Advent wreath (See First Sunday of Advent—Cycle A for instructions on how to make and use.)

Baker's Clay
2 cups flour
½ cup salt
¾ cup water
Mix and knead. Cool.
Roll to approximately ⅛ inch.
Cut in desired shapes.
Bake 350°F.

Discuss
Sunday Advent begins. Advent is a special time when we should be getting ready for Jesus' birthday. How do we get ready for Christmas? (Let the students tell about their Christmas preparations. If one tells about Christmas decorations, say: "Yes, we always decorate for a special celebration, so we decorate the house at Christmas to celebrate Jesus' birthday." When someone mentions

gift exchange, say: "God loves us so very much he gave us the gift of his only son, Jesus. To show others our love we give them gifts. But no gift is as great as the one God gave us, Jesus.")

Lesson
Advent is the season to watch and prepare for Jesus' coming. That is also what Jesus is saying in the gospel. Jesus told his followers that no one knows when Jesus will come again. Like a man who goes on a trip and leaves his servants [his workers] to do their work. They must keep busy, doing as the master [boss] asks so when the master returns he will find them ready for him.

That is why we spend Advent preparing for the day we will meet Jesus face to face.

Liturgy
On altar have the Bible with an Advent wreath. Gather around the altar. Light one candle on the Advent wreath. All join hands.

All:
Lord, make us turn to you; let us see your face and we shall be saved. Come, Lord Jesus, into our hearts. Help us to prepare for your coming. Lord, make us turn to you; let us see your face and we shall be saved.

Activity
Baker's clay: Give each student a piece about the size of a tennis ball. Have the students roll out to about ⅛ inch thick (like cookie dough thickness). Use Christmas cookie cutters for star, angel, and any other religious symbols, or use cardboard patterns and have students cut out with a table knife. Roll dough scraps in hands to form shepherd's crook. Have students place cutouts on grocery sack which is laying flat. With round toothpick, make a whole near the top of each cutout for hanging.

Note to Teacher

Sacks stack flat and are easy to transport home. Bake at 350°F. Bake each student's separately, then place inside sack for next class.

Letter to Parents

Dear Parents,

We are beginning Advent, a time of preparation for Christ's birth, as all our lives should be a time of preparation for the com-ing of Christ. Make an Advent wreath to burn during your family prayer time. Instructions are attached.

Sincerely in Christ,
Teacher _____

Questions

Whose birthday do we celebrate at Christmas?

We get ready for Christmas in a special way. Should we always be ready to meet Jesus?

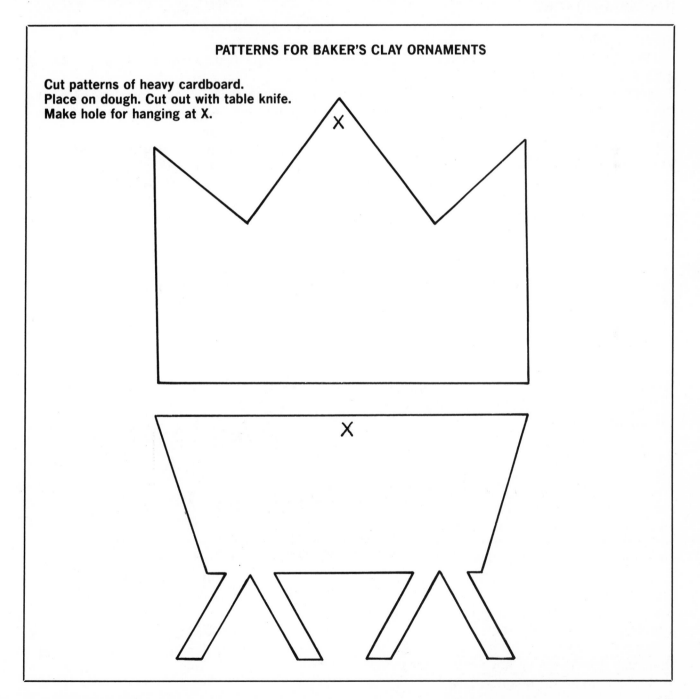

PATTERNS FOR BAKER'S CLAY ORNAMENTS

Cut patterns of heavy cardboard.
Place on dough. Cut out with table knife.
Make hole for hanging at X.

Cycle B
Second Sunday of Advent

When I Am Sorry, God Forgives Me

Supplies Needed
honey
tempera paint
paste brushes
glitter
1 plastic spoon per student
paint brushes or Q tips
glue
yarn or silver or gold braid
cut into 3-inch lengths

Begin class by giving each student a teaspoon of honey. Smell it—feel it—taste it.

Lesson
Once there was a man named John the Baptist, who lived in the desert and ate grasshoppers and honey. He told everyone to repent [be sorry for your sins] and be baptized with water for forgiveness. Then he told them someone greater than he was coming. This someone was so great John the Baptist was not worthy to untie his sandals. Can anyone tell me who John the Baptist was talking about? [Jesus]

Liturgy
Light two candles of Advent wreath. Explain the psalm: This Is a Way to Ask God to Forgive Us. Sit in a circle around altar. Cover eyes with your hands. Quietly think about any wrong things we have done. (Pause.) Join hands and say together: Dear Jesus, I am sorry for every wrong I have done. Please forgive me. Lord, let us see your kindness and grant us your salvation. (Exchange a greeting of peace with each other.)

Teacher: Whenever we have made our peace with God and our neighbor, we should be filled with joy. Let us share that joy in song as we sing: "Joy, Joy, Joy" (from "Hi God" record).

Activity
Complete tree ornaments by painting with tempera paint. When dry, paint again with glue and roll in glitter. (Use a clear-drying, non-toxic glue.) Run yard or braid through hole and tie so ornament can be hung on tree. Sing while finishing ornaments.

Letter to Parents
Dear Parents,
  Light the second candle of your Advent wreath.
  Today our theme was repentance. In your family prayers, include a simple act of contrition. In class today our prayer was, "Dear Jesus, I am sorry for every wrong I have done. Please forgive me."
      Sincerely in Christ,
      Teacher _____

Questions
When we do wrong, should we say, "I am sorry"?
Does God forgive us when we say, "I am sorry"?

Cycle B
Third Sunday of Advent

We Must Say "I Am Sorry" to Be Forgiven

Supplies Needed
heart drawn on red construction paper,
1 per student, plus a few extra to replace any that get damaged.
(Pattern on page 51)
stickers of the head of Jesus
pins
scissors

Lesson

Last week we talked about John the Baptist. [Encourage the students to tell you what they remember about last week's lesson. Fill in the parts they have forgotten.] The leaders of the people sent some men to John the Baptist to ask, "Who are you?"

John said, "I am not the Christ."

"Then who are you?" they asked.

John said, "I am a voice in the desert crying out, 'Make straight the way of the Lord.'" [That was another way to tell people to repent of their sins.] But the men did not give up. Now they asked, "If you are not the Christ why do you baptize?" John said, "I baptize with water but standing here with you is one you do not know. His sandals I am unworthy to untie." [Who was John talking about? Jesus.]

Discuss

It is not easy to say "I was wrong. I am sorry." But we must say it if we want to know Jesus and have Jesus come into our heart.

Liturgy

Sit in a circle around altar. Light three candles on the Advent wreath. Cover eyes with hands. In silence think about any wrongs we have done. (Pause.) Join hands and say together: Dear Jesus, I am sorry for every wrong I have done. Please forgive me. Come into my heart. [Pause.] All say together: My soul rejoices in my God. Sing: "Silent Night."

Activity

Cut out red construction paper hearts. Place seal of Jesus in center. Let each student cut out pre-drawn heart. Have some hearts already cut out for any student who is unhappy with his/her own cut work. Pin heart on each student.

Letter to Parents

Dear Parents,

Light three candles of your Advent wreath, two purple and the rose.

Again today, our theme is repentance. Continue to include a simple act of contrition in your family prayer time.

Sincerely in Christ,
Teacher _____

Note to Teacher

If next week is Christmas vacation, add: N.B. Next week is Christmas vacation. Beginning with the Sunday of that week, light all four candles of your Advent wreath.

Questions

Is it easy to say, "I am sorry"?
Does God forgive us when we say, "I am sorry"?

Have one heart per student in red construction paper. Make a few extra in case students have trouble cutting their own.

Cycle B
Fourth Sunday of Advent

Jesus Is God's Greatest Gift to Us

Supplies Needed
pictures of Jesus as a man
small boxes
gift tags
pens
gift wrap
glue
scissors

Begin lesson by teaching the first part of the Hail Mary with gestures. (See this page.) After students know it, say it all together slowly, then go right into the gospel story.

Lesson
The angel Gabriel was sent from God to a town of Galilee named Nazareth, to a virgin engaged to a man named Joseph. The virgin's name was Mary. "Rejoice, O highly favored daughter! [Hail Mary, full of grace] The Lord is with you. Blessed are you among women." The angel went on to say to her. "Do not fear, Mary. You have found favor with God. You shall conceive and bear a son and give him the name Jesus."

Liturgy
Gather around altar. Light all four candles on the Advent wreath. All say: Forever I will sing the goodness of the Lord. Add the Hail Mary with gestures.

Discuss
At Christmas we give gifts. Why do we give gifts at Christmas? (To show our love.) What is the greatest gift you ever received? After each student has named what they feel is their greatest gift, say to them: God has given us a greater gift than any you have named. Can anyone think what it is? [Try to draw from them the response, "Jesus."] Jesus is God's greatest gift to us.

Activity
Have students paste a picture of Jesus (the man) in the bottom of a box. Gift-wrap the box. Make a tag for the box that reads, "God's greatest gift to my family." (Students take home to share with their families.)

Letter to Parents
Dear Parents,
Light all the candles on the Advent wreath. Ask your child to share the gift box brought home from class today. Include in your prayer time a prayer of thanks for so great a gift.

Sincerely in Christ,
Teacher _____

Questions
Do we give gifts at Christmas because we love others?
Who has given us the greatest gift of all? (God)
What was God's great gift to us? (Jesus)

Hail Mary Gestures
Hail Mary (right hand raised as if to wave)
Full of grace (arms crossed on chest)
The Lord (arms and hands raised heavenward)
Is with you. (hands extended straight ahead)
Blessed are you (arms crossed on chest)
Among women (arms spread wide)
And blessed is the fruit
of your womb (arms crossed on chest)
Jesus. (with arms still crossed, bow head)

Cycle B
First Sunday of Year

Jesus Is God's Son

Supplies Needed
matching cards (see pattern, page 53; instructions, page 2)

Review

In some of our lessons before Christmas we talked about John the Baptist. (See how much the students remember.) John told the people to repent (be sorry for their sins or wrongs). When the people repented, he baptized them with water. He also said that someone would be coming whose sandal John was not worthy to untie. Whom did he mean? (Jesus.)

Lesson

One day while John was baptizing the people Jesus came to be baptized also. When Jesus came out of the water the sky opened and the Holy Spirit came down in the form of a dove and a voice from the clouds said, "You are my beloved son. On you my favor rests."

Activity

Dove-shaped matching cards. Words: Jesus is God's son.

Visit the baptistry in the church. Or make arrangements ahead of time for students to witness a baptism. Your priest may be willing to schedule one during your class hour.

Liturgy

Gather around altar. Join hands.

All:

The Lord will bless his people with peace. Jesus, when I tell you I am sorry, you forgive me and bless me with your peace. [All exchange a greeting of peace saying: The peace of Christ be with you.]

Letter to Parents

Dear Parents,

Today we discussed the peace that follows repentance. In your family prayer this week, include the psalm: The Lord Will Bless His People with Peace. End by exchanging a greeting of peace.

Sincerely in Christ,
Teacher _____

Questions

Who is God's Son? (Jesus)
Is Jesus God's Son? (Yes)

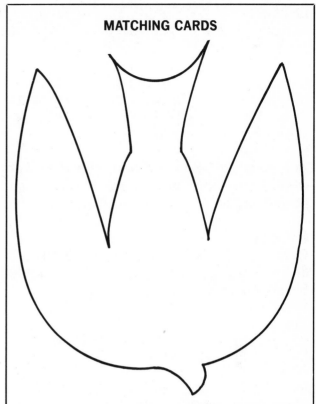

MATCHING CARDS

Cut 8 per student. Words: JESUS IS GOD'S SON
To use
Teacher or helper lays out first set in order, and repeats aloud, if student cannot read; or have student read. Student then matches second set to first set and reads aloud.

Cycle B
Second Sunday of Year

Jesus Is Our Best Friend

Supplies Needed

1 sheet poster board
½ sheet construction paper per student
1 sheet construction paper per student
1 medium-sized picture of Jesus as a man
1 small picture of Jesus as a man,
per student (greeting card size)
crayola
glue
marking pens

Lesson

The day after John baptized Jesus, John saw Jesus passing by. "Look, there goes the Lamb of God." When John's friends heard this they started to follow Jesus. Jesus turned around, saw them following him and said, "What do you want?" They answered, "Teacher, where do you live?"

Jesus said, "Come and see." So they went with Jesus and saw where he lived and stayed the rest of the day with Jesus.

Discuss

Can you imagine spending a whole day with Jesus? Do you like to spend a day at a good friend's house? Jesus is our best friend.

Liturgy

Gather around altar. All say: Here am I, Lord: I come to do your will.

Sing: "Jesus Loves Me," using gestures:
Jesus loves me this I know
   (hug self)
For the Bible tells me so
   (hands form open book)
Little ones to him belong
   (hands and arms outstretched)
We are weak (go all limp)
But he is strong
   (arms up, show off muscle)
Yes, Jesus loves me
   (nod yes and hug self)
Yes, Jesus loves me
   (nod yes and hug self)
Yes, Jesus loves me
   (nod yes and hug self)
The Bible tells me so
   (hands form open book)

Sing: Jesus, Jesus
Jesus, in the morning
Jesus, in the noontime
Jesus, Jesus
Jesus, when the sun goes down.

Activity

Have a sheet of poster board with a picture of Jesus as a man, in the center. Print on the poster board "Jesus and His Friends." Have each student draw a picture of him/herself on the ½ sheet of construction paper and write their names on it. Paste it on the poster board.

Give each student a piece of 9″ x 12″ construction paper and a picture of Jesus. (If using pictures from old greeting cards, avoid baby Jesus and the boy Jesus.) Have students paste Jesus on the construction paper and print the words "My Best Friend." Encourage them to put the picture on the wall in their room at home.

Letter to Parents

Dear Parents,

   This week, speak often with your child about good friends and the importance of friendship. Stress that Jesus is the best friend we all have.

Sincerely in Christ,
Teacher _____

Questions

Is Jesus our best friend?
Are we a friend to Jesus?
Does Jesus love us?
Do you love Jesus?

Cycle B
Third Sunday of Year

Jesus Teaches Us

Supplies Needed

Matching cards (see pattern and instructions, pages 56 and 2)
4 fish shapes per student
2 plastic soda straws per student
1 spool black thread
scissors
box round toothpicks
needle

Discuss

Fishing. Ask if anyone has ever gone fishing. Let the students tell about it. Question them so they describe how to fish. Then explain that in Jesus' day fishermen used nets. Some fishermen who make their living catching fish today still use nets.

Lesson
One day Jesus was walking by the Sea of Galilee. He saw two fishermen named Simon and his brother Andrew, casting their net into the sea. Jesus said, "Come, follow me and I will make you fishers of men." A little farther along he saw James and John with their father Zebedee. They were in their boat mending their nets. Jesus called to James and John and they left their father with his workers and followed Jesus, also.

Now Jesus has chosen his first apostles [friends] to do his work. That work is to bring all people to know God but before the apostles can do this Jesus must teach them. That is what Jesus meant when he said, "I will make you fishers of men." The apostles would learn to bring others to God.

Liturgy
Gather around altar. Join hands.

All:
Teach me your ways, O Lord.

Sing:
Jesus, Jesus,
Jesus, in the morning
Jesus, in the noontime
Jesus, Jesus,
Jesus, when the sun goes down.
Teach me, teach me,
Teach me in the morning
Teach me in the noontime
Teach me, teach me,
Teach me when the sun goes down.

Activity
Fish-shaped matching cards:

Apostles were Jesus' friends and helpers.
They told others about Jesus.
He wants me for a friend.

(See instructions to make and use, page 56.)
Fish mobile (pattern and instructions, page 56.)

Letter to Parents
Dear Parents,
Include in your family prayers this week, "Teach me your ways, O Lord."
In your discussions with your child about Jesus, our best friend, encourage your child to talk to Jesus as he/she talks to his/her other friends.

Sincerely in Christ,
Teacher _____

Questions
Who were the Apostles? (Jesus' friends)
Did Jesus teach the Apostles?
Should we learn about Jesus also?

Cycle B
Fourth Sunday of Year

Appreciation of Our Health and Concern for Others

Supplies needed
lined paper
construction paper
crayolas
pens
envelopes
postage stamps

Lesson
One day Jesus was teaching in the temple [church] when a man came in who had a devil living in him. When he saw Jesus, the devil in him called out, "What do you want with us? Have you come to destroy us? I know who you are: The Holy One of God." Jesus said sharply, "Be quiet! Come out of him." The devil threw the man on the floor and made him sick, then left him.

The people were all surprised to see even the devil had to obey Jesus.

Discuss
Can you imagine how happy that man was to be made well by Jesus? That man suffered

FISH MOBILE:
Give each student 4 fish cutouts.
Fold fish in half lengthwise. (Fig. 1)
Clip along fold as shown. (Fig. 2)
Unfold and weave round toothpick through slashes. (Fig. 3)
Run a thread through a plastic drinking straw.
Tie a fish on each end.
Repeat with second straw.
Tie straws together. (Fig. 4)
fold

Matching Card Instructions
1. Cut out fish shapes, 2 for each word. (34 fish)
2. Print only one word on a card.
3. Make two cards for each word.
4. Color code the cards. (i.e.: word APOSTLES
same color; word WERE another color,
etc. This allows the non-reader to participate.)
5. Teacher lays one set of cards out in order shown, saying the words aloud.
6. Turn second set face down. Students choose a fish.

APOSTLES	THEY	HE
WERE	TOLD	WANTS
JESUS'	OTHERS	ME
FRIENDS	ABOUT	FOR
AND	JESUS	A
HELPERS		FRIEND

FRIENDS
7. Students match words in order.

Pattern for matching cards and fish mobile. (Pattern shows completed fish for mobile.)

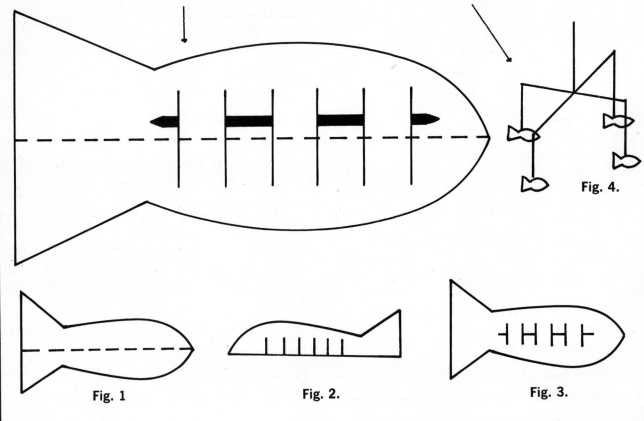

Fig. 1   Fig. 2.   Fig. 3.

Fig. 4.

from something much worse than anything any of us has ever suffered. Think how happy we are just to get well from a cold.

Liturgy
Gather around altar. Join hands.

All:
If today you hear his voice, harden not your hearts.

Teacher:
We want Jesus to always live in our hearts.

All:
Come to me, Lord Jesus.

(Ask students to name any sick person they would like to pray for.)

All:
Jesus, please make our friends well. Thank you, Jesus, for making people well again.

Sing:
"Joy, Joy, Joy" from "Hi God" (all verses).

Activity
Encourage the students to think again of the people in the nursing home. Have them write letters and/or draw pictures for their lonely sick friends. (See thirty-fourth Sunday of Year, Cycle A.)

Letter to Parents
Dear Parents,
    In your prayers this week, remember the sick and lonely. If you know a shut in or a lonely person, take your child for a short visit to that person.

                                    Sincerely in Christ,
                                    Teacher _____

Questions
Can Jesus cure (make well) the sick?
Should we pray for our sick relatives and friends?
Should we thank Jesus when someone gets better?

Cycle B
Fifth Sunday of Year

Introduction to Quiet Prayer

Lesson
Jesus went with James and John to stay at Peter and Andrew's house. Peter's mother-in-law was sick in bed with a fever. Jesus went in to see her. He took her by the hand and she got well immediately. When people heard this they started to bring all the sick people to Jesus to make them well. Very early the next morning Jesus got up and went out to a lonely place to pray.

Activity
Act out the story.

Discuss
(When students finish acting out the story.)

Even Jesus liked to be in a quiet, lonely place to pray. Today we are going to do quiet prayer.

Liturgy
Sit on chairs around the altar. Place hands over eyes.

Teacher:
Let us tell God quietly all about ourselves and what is in our hearts. (Give the students several minutes of quiet prayer.) End by saying: Praise the Lord who heals the broken-hearted.

Sing:
"Praise God" to tune "Amazing Grace." Repeat the words "Praise God" throughout the entire song.

Letter to Parents
Dear Parents,
    Jesus liked to go off by himself to pray.
    In class this week we had quiet prayer.

Each person spoke to God quietly in his/her heart. Include a moment or two of silent prayer in your family prayer time this week.

Sincerely in Christ,
Teacher _____

Questions

Did Jesus like to go off to a quiet place to pray?

Can we pray to Jesus quietly in our hearts?

Cycle B
Sixth Sunday of Year

When We Pray Jesus Listens to Us We Must Also Listen to Jesus

Supplies Needed

paper to tear and crumple
ball to bounce
glass of water and an empty glass
other items for listening game

Activity

Play a listening game.

Have a helper out of sight of the students make noises for the students to identify. Example: Clap hands; stamp feet; snap fingers; tear paper; crumple paper; bounce ball; pour water; etc.

Lesson

A leper [a man with an incurable skin disease] came to Jesus and on his knees he said, "If you want to, you can cure me [make me well]." Jesus said, "Yes, I want to be cured" [be made well]. Immediately the man was cured. Jesus told the man, "Go show yourself to the priest but do not tell anyone about your cure." But as the man went on his way he told everyone about his recovery. Soon Jesus could no longer go freely about for everyone was coming to him.

Stress

Jesus listened to this man when he asked to be cured, but did the man listen to Jesus?

Liturgy

Gather around altar.

Teacher:

When we pray, Jesus listens to us. We must also listen to Jesus. Today we are going to pray quietly as we did last week. (Have students cover eyes and quietly tell Jesus what is in their hearts.) After several minutes, say: Now listen to Jesus. (Stay quiet again for several minutes.) End with:

All:

I turn to you, Lord, in time of trouble, and you fill me with the joy of salvation.

If time permits, repeat activity.

Letter to Parents

Dear Parents,

Part of praying is listening to God. To help your child develop his/her power of concentration and ability to listen, have your child stop periodically to listen for a few minutes, then tell you what he/she heard in the sounds around him/her. Gradually lengthen the listening time. For this to be effective you, too, must stop and listen with your child.

Sincerely in Christ,
Teacher _____

Questions

When we pray, does Jesus listen to us?

Should we take time to listen to Jesus?

**Cycle B
Seventh Sunday of Year**

We Ask God's Forgiveness and Thank God For His Forgiveness

Supplies Needed
1 large grocery sack per student
scissors
crayolas

Lesson
One day Jesus was teaching the people at his home. So many people had come to hear Jesus there was no room left for anyone else to get in. Four men had a sick friend who was paralyzed [could not move at all]. They carried their sick friend on a pallet [stretcher] to the house where Jesus was teaching. It was so crowded they could not get in, but that did not stop them. They went up on the roof and made a hole in the roof and let their friend down through the roof to Jesus.

Seeing their faith [their belief in Jesus], Jesus said, "Your sins are forgiven."

Some of the people when they heard Jesus, said, "How can he forgive sins; only God can forgive sins?" When Jesus heard them he said, "So you will know that the Son of Man [a name he called himself] has the power to forgive sins." Then he said to the sick man, "Rise, take your pallet [stretcher] and go home." The sick man got up, picked up his pallet and went home.

Liturgy
Gather around altar.

All:
Lord, heal my soul for I have sinned against you.

(Have students make up an act of contrition. Have students make up a prayer thanking God for his forgiveness.)

All:
Lord, heal my soul for I have sinned against you.

Activity
Make a house with a hole in roof.

Use one large grocery sack per student.

Cut sack in two.

Use bottom portion for house.

Invert. See diagram.

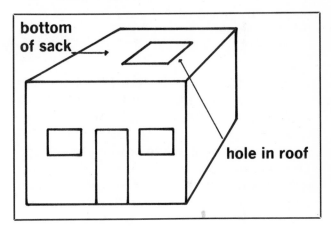

Students draw door, windows, and cut hole in roof.

Color.

Letter to Parents
Dear Parents,
This week, include in your family prayers the psalm, "Lord, Heal My Soul For I Have Sinned against You." Add a prayer of thanks for God's mercy and forgiveness.
Sincerely in Christ,
Teacher _____

Questions
Can God forgive our sins?
Does God forgive our sins when we say, "I am sorry"?
Should we thank God for forgiving us?

Cycle B
Eighth Sunday of Year

To Know Jesus Is Always With Us, Yet, Comes In a Special Way In the Eucharist

Supplies Needed
3″ × 5″ lined index card,
one per student (see Activity)
pens or pencils

Lesson
In Jesus' day people fasted. [Went for long periods of time without food. Can you imagine how hungry you would be if when you get home from class today your mother or father would say you could have nothing to eat until dinner tomorrow?] People fasted because they thought that would better prepare them for God. Jesus' disciples [followers] did not fast. One day some people came to Jesus and complained. They asked, "Why do John's disciples and those of the Pharisees [leaders of the people] fast and your disciples do not?"

Jesus answered them with one of his riddles. "How can guests at a wedding fast as long as the groom is still with them?" [Remember, we said people fasted to prepare themselves to meet God. But Jesus is God. His disciples did not need to prepare to meet God. He was already with them.]

Discuss
When do we meet Jesus? (Encourage the students to answer with times and places. Answers may include any place they go or time they name. Hopefully, their answers will include: "in my heart"; "at prayer"; "in church"; "at Mass"; and in "Holy Communion.")

How do we prepare to meet Jesus in Holy Communion? (Besides such answers as proper grooming before going to Mass, draw out "praying" and "being good.")

Activity
Have students name ways to be good by doing something for others. Stand in a circle and sing with gestures (tune: "Mulberry Bush"):

This is the way I'll make my bed,
Make my bed, make my bed,
This is the way I'll make my bed
As Jesus wants me to.

(Sing a verse for each good deed students name.)

Have 3″ × 5″ lined index cards on which is printed:

This week, every day I will

Each student finishes sentence with a good deed or a special prayer. Student takes card home to parents.

Liturgy
Gather around altar. Join hands. Close eyes.

Leader:
Jesus, you are Lord.

All:
The Lord is kind and merciful.

Leader:
Jesus, you are in my heart.

All:
The Lord is kind and merciful.

Leader:
Jesus, you are everywhere I go.

All:
The Lord is kind and merciful.

Leader:
Jesus, help me to do good.

All:
The Lord is kind and merciful.

Leader:
Thank you, Jesus, for coming to me
in Holy Communion.

All:
The Lord is kind and merciful.

Letter to Parents
Dear Parents,
Jesus is always with us, yet he comes to us in a special way at Communion; therefore, we prepare to meet him. The good deed on the card your child brings home today is his/her choice. Encourage him/her to do it each day.
Sincerely in Christ,
Teacher _____

Questions
Is Jesus everywhere?
Is Jesus always with us?
When does Jesus come to us in a special way?
(In Holy Communion.)

Cycle B
Ninth Sunday of Year

Keep Holy the Lord's Day

Supplies Needed
crayolas
scissors
glue
church cutout (1 per student)
See pattern, page 63.

Lesson
One day as Jesus was walking through a field of grain on the Sabbath [a day of prayer like our Sunday] his disciples began to pull off heads of grain as they went along. At this the Pharisees [leaders of the people] objected. "Look! Why do you do a thing not permitted on the Sabbath?" Jesus said, "Have you never read what David did when he was in need and his men hungry? [David was a man of God who had lived long before Jesus.] David entered God's house and ate the holy bread. He even gave some to his men. The Sabbath was made for man, not man for the Sabbath."

Discuss
It was wrong for the people to work on the Sabbath day. When the disciples picked some grain to eat, the Pharisees accused them of working. But Jesus reminded them of David, a holy man they all admired. David had done what was thought to be wrong when he and his men were hungry. David entered the house of God and fed his men with the holy bread.

Stress
God gave us a commandment (law) that says "Keep holy the Lord's day."

What day is the Lord's day? (Sunday)

How do we keep it holy? (By going to Mass and not working)

If students are unable to answer the questions, rephrase them as follows:

Is Sunday the Lord's day?

Do we keep Sunday holy by going to Mass?

Do we keep Sunday holy by not working?

Of course there is some work we must do on Sunday. Mother or father cooks our meals. We make our beds and do the dishes. Some mothers and fathers have to go to work on Sundays, too.

This is what Jesus was telling the Pharisees. His disciples had to eat so it was necessary to pick the grain.

Liturgy
Gather around the altar.

Teacher:
At Mass, we say a special prayer to God. In it we say, "Thy will be done." That means we want to do the things God wants us to do. One of these things is to keep holy the Lord's day.

All:
Say or sing the Lord's Prayer with gestures.

THE LORD'S PRAYER
Our Father (right hand on heart)

Who art in heaven (both hands raised heavenward)

Hallowed be thy name (hands folded across chest, head bowed)

Thy kingdom (hands extended forward and raised, look up to heaven)

Come (bring hands to chest)

Thy will be done (hands extended forward and raised)

On earth (hands and arms move in opposite directions in a circular motion)

As it is in heaven. (hands come together at completion of circle and raise heavenward)

Give us this day our daily bread (hands cupped and extended forward as if receiving something)

And forgive us our trespasses as we forgive those who trespass against us (hands folded and head bowed)

And lead us *not* into temptation (*not* emphasized and on the word "not" hands are extended as though pushing something away)

But deliver us from evil. (hands raised to right side as if warding off something)

For the kingdom (hands and arms move in opposite directions in a circular motion)

And the power (repeat circular motion with hands and arms raised slightly)

And the glory (raise hands and arms higher and repeat circular motion)

Are yours (raise hands and arms heavenward)

Now and forever. (arms folded across chest)

Amen. (fold hands and bow head)

Note to Teacher: Practice gestures yourself ahead of class so they become natural to you.

Activity
Make a church (see pattern and instructions, page 63).

Letter to Parents
Dear Parents,
Include in your family prayer the Lord's Prayer. Use the gestures so it will be more meaningful to your child. Gestures attached.
Sincerely in Christ,
Teacher _____

Questions
What day is the Lord's day?
Must we keep the Lord's day holy?
How do we keep the Lord's day holy?

1. Make one per student of tag board.
2. Cut all lines marked cut, before class.
3. Students color church.
4. Glue A onto B, each end.
5. Fold C to glue line on A, and glue, each end.
6. Fold D to glue line on A and glue, each end.

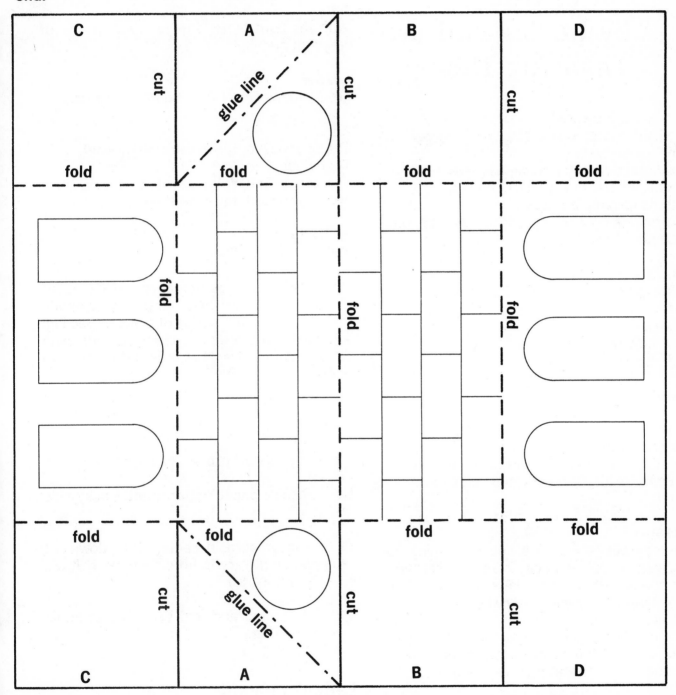

Cycle B
Tenth Sunday of Year

We Do the Will of God by Loving and Thanking Him

Supplies Needed
¼ sheet poster board (11″ × 14″) per student
one world and one praying hands
cutout per student (pattern, page 65)
cutouts of birds and food
(approximately size of world and hands), one each per student
glue
pencils
marking pens
scissors
crayolas
clear adhesive shelf paper
(13″ × 16″) per student

Discuss
We have learned that God in heaven is Jesus' Father. God in heaven is our Father. (All say the Our Father with gestures.) That makes Jesus our brother, but in today's lesson Jesus tells us it takes more to be his brother or sister.

Lesson
One day Jesus was in a house teaching all the many people who had come to hear him. His mother and all his relatives came to see him. The house was so crowded they could not get in. When Jesus was told his mother and relatives were waiting outside to see him, he said, "Whoever does the will of God is brother, sister and mother to me."

Stress
The will of God is doing what God wants. How do we do the will of God?

We love everyone. We love God. We try always to be good. We praise and thank God for everything.

Liturgy
Gather around altar.

All:
With the Lord there is mercy and fullness of redemption.

Leader:
Let us thank God for all he has given us.

All:
Thank you God, for the world so sweet.
Thank you God, for the food we eat.
Thank you God, for the birds that sing.
Thank you God, for everything.

Activity
Make prayer cards.

On ¼ sheet of poster board each student glues a world, food, birds, and praying hands to correspond with words of prayer. (See Fig. 1.) Have cards pre-printed for students who cannot copy prayer. Let others do their own work.

Cover completed cards with clear adhesive shelf paper.

Student peels off protective paper.

Lay adhesive paper flat on table, sticky side up.

Place prayer card in center, face down. (If crooked, do NOT try to lift off adhesive. It will ruin the art work.)

Cut out corners and fold back excess adhesive paper (Fig. 2).

Letter to Parents
Dear Parents,
   Your child is bringing home a prayer card today. Use the prayer as a grace before

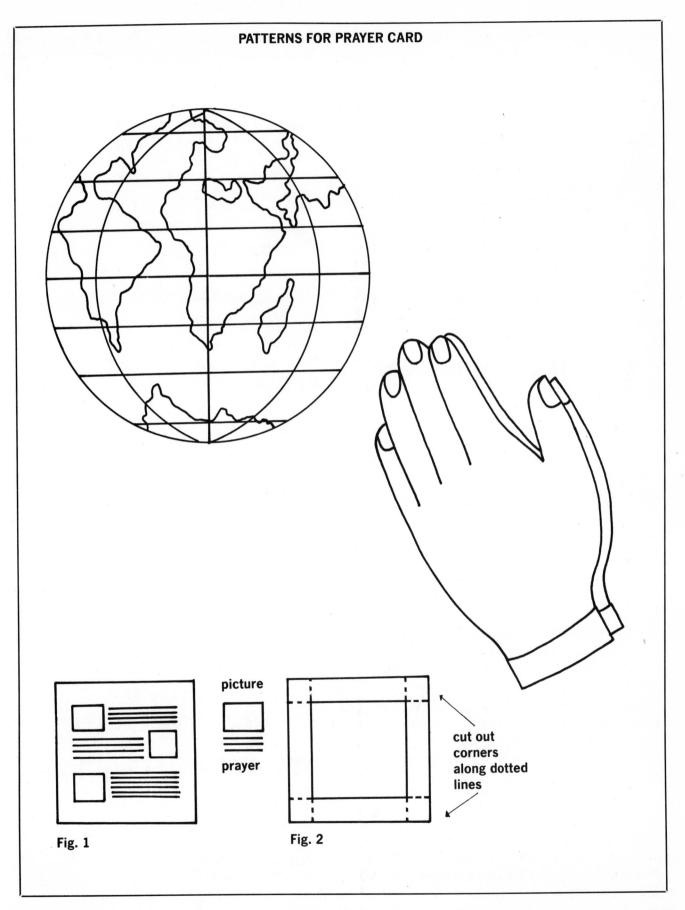

picture

prayer

Fig. 1

Fig. 2

cut out
corners
along dotted
lines

meals or as a special "thank you" to God at your family prayer time.

Sincerely in Christ,
Teacher _____

Questions:
Should we always do what God wants?
Does God want us to love him?
Does God want us to love everyone?
Does God want us to thank him?

Cycle B
Eleventh Sunday of Year

We Thank the Lord and Celebrate Our Year Together

Supplies Needed
picture of tree   mustard seeds
napkins   cookies or graham crackers
cups   juice

Note to Teacher: Have mustard seeds so students can see how small they are. (Can be purchased in the spice section of a grocery store.) Let students taste the seeds.

Lesson
Today Jesus talks about the "Reign of God." He is talking about God's kingdom, that is, all the people who will come to hear about God and believe in him.

Jesus said, "The Reign of God is like a mustard seed. It is very small but when it is planted in the soil it will grow into a large shrub [tree] that even the birds will build their nests in its branches."

Discuss
Summer vacation begins soon. We have heard a lot about God this school year. During our summer vacation we will let God's love grow in us, just as the mustard seed will grow into a tree.

Liturgy
Gather around altar. Join hands.

Teacher:
Let us thank God for our wonderful year together. [Have each student mention something about the school year that he/she is thankful for.) After each, all respond with: Lord, it is good to give thanks to you.

Teacher:
Please, God, may we all be together again next year.

All:
Lord, it is good to give thanks to you.

Activity
Have a party to celebrate your year together. Sing all the students' favorite songs about God.

Letter to Parents
Dear Parents,
We have enjoyed having (student's name) in class this year. We are looking forward to seeing him/her again in the fall. Wishing you and your family a joyful summer vacation.

Sincerely in Christ,
Teacher _____

Questions
Does God love us?
Do we love God?
Will we let God's love grow in us?

Cycle B
First Sunday of Lent

We Reform Our Lives

Supplies Needed
12" × 18" sheet construction paper, one per student
Prepare as directed in activity on page 67, 68 before class.
Stickers of nature; Christ; cross, etc.

Lesson

After Jesus spent 40 days in the desert praying, he went about the country telling everyone the good news. Jesus said, "God is near. Reform your lives [begin to be better] and believe the good news." (The Good News was Jesus had come to save us.)

Discuss

Ways students can reform their lives. Encourage them to tell you the ways they can improve. Suggestions: Do my chores cheerfully. Do my chores promptly. Always be polite. Try harder to succeed. Offer to help others.

Liturgy

Gather around the altar. Have each of the students again repeat their way to reform their lives by saying, "Dear Jesus, I will try to [name the way they will try to improve.]" After each all respond with: Your ways, O Lord, are love and truth, to those who keep your covenant [law].

Activity

Make a Lenten calendar.

Each student is given a sheet of 12″ × 18″ construction paper that has been prepared ahead of class. Students enter the month and days of week at the top. Enter the dates in the upper left-hand corner of each square, beginning with Ash Wednesday. Each day of Lent after the student has done his /her chores cheerfully and promptly, he/she adds a sticker to that date on their calendar. (Stickers can be cross cut of black sticky paper, available at stationery stores; head of Christ and other meaningful religious stickers found in church goods stores; and nature stickers for creation.)

Letter to Parents

Dear Parents,

Your child is bringing home a Lenten calendar.

Everyday he/she is to place a sticker on the calendar after doing his/her chores cheerfully and promptly.

Sincerely in Christ,
Teacher _____

Questions

Does Jesus want us to be better people? Should we try every day to be better? Does the Good News mean that Jesus came to save us?

Cycle B
Second Sunday of Lent

We Listen to Jesus

Supplies Needed

large box
balloon
paper to tear or crumple
empty glass
bell
ball
glass of water

Activity

Play listening game.

Have a helper out of sight of students or working behind a large box make noises for students to identify. Example: tear and crumple paper; ring bell; pop balloon; bounce a ball; pour water; snap fingers; clap hands; etc.

Lesson

One day Jesus took three of his apostles [his friends] up a high mountain. Here he was changed before them. His clothes were dazzling white. So bright they could hardly look at him. Two prophets [men who lived long before Jesus and told of his coming on earth] appeared and talked with Jesus. A cloud appeared. Out of the cloud a voice said, "This is my son, my beloved. Listen to him." Suddenly the apostles looked around and no one was there—only Jesus.

Discuss

Listening to Jesus. When we listen to Jesus we try to do better.

LENTEN CALENDAR:

Use one sheet 12" × 18" construction paper per student.

All lines and printing should be done in purple.

1. Starting at left edge of 12" side, rule off 6 columns 1¾" wide (7th column is 1½" wide).

2. Starting at left edge of 18" side, rule off 9 columns 2" wide.

3. Divide first left-hand 2" column into two 1" columns.

4. Turn page so top is 12" wide. In second 1" row, enter the days of the week.

5. Enter month name above week days.

6. Above steps should all be done before class.

7. Students enter dates in upper left-hand corner of each box. Begin with Ash Wednesday.

8. Enter month name when date changes to new month.

9. End with Easter Sunday.

10. Pencil in dates ahead for students who are unable to do their own. Have them trace the numbers in purple.

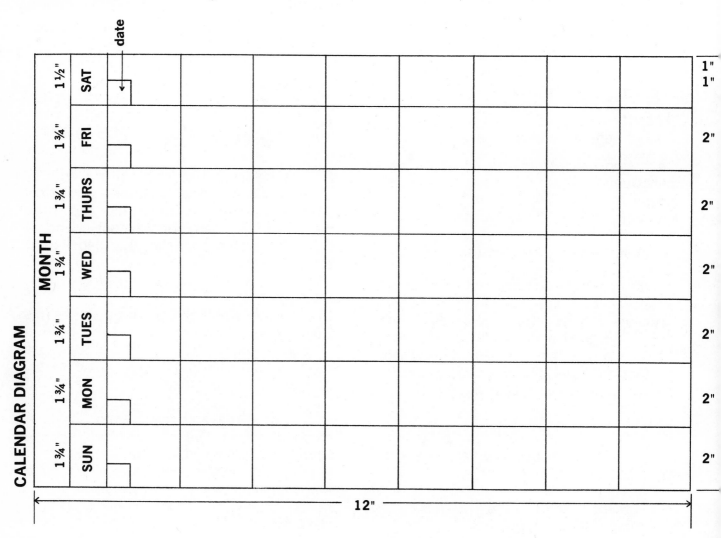

CALENDAR DIAGRAM

68

Liturgy

Explain the psalm: In Heaven We Will Walk with Jesus as the Apostles did in today's lesson.

Gather around altar. Close eyes.

All:
I will walk in the presence of the Lord, in the land of the living.

Take time for quiet prayer. Encourage students to talk quietly to God, then listen to God. Close with:

All:
I will walk in the presence of the Lord, in the land of the living.

Letter to Parents

Dear Parents,

Encourage your child to continue his/her Lenten calendar. Spend part of your family prayer time in silence, listening to Jesus.

Sincerely in Christ,
Teacher _____

Questions

Can we listen to Jesus?
Does Jesus tell us to be a better person?
Should we try each day to be better?

Cycle B
Third Sunday of Lent

Jesus Is Our Savior

Supplies Needed

poster board cut in fourths (¼ per student)
pictures of Jesus as a man (one per student)
glue
glitter
paint brushes
tissue paper
colored paper
scissors
paints
crayolas
felt pens

Lesson

Jesus went to the temple [church] to pray. In the temple entrance people were selling oxen [cattle], sheep and doves. Others were changing money for people. Jesus made a whip of cords and drove them all out of the temple. He turned over the tables of coins [money]. He told them, "Get out of here. Stop turning my father's house into a market place" [a place where things are bought and sold]. Who was Jesus' father? [God]. We call the Church, "God's house."

Some people asked Jesus to show them a sign that he had the right to do these things. Jesus said, "Destroy this temple and in three days I will raise it up." [People did not understand Jesus for they thought he was talking about the church building, but he meant that three days after he died and was buried he would rise again from the dead.]

Discuss

It was hard for the people to understand Jesus. They did not know he was God's Son who had come to die for them and would be raised from the dead three days later. Isn't it wonderful that we know Jesus did this for us? Now we can go to heaven. That is what our prayer today means when we say, "Lord, you have the words of everlasting life." (End with a prayer of thanksgiving to Jesus for being our Savior.)

Liturgy

Gather around altar. Join hands. Have students make up acts of contrition. After each student says an act of contrition all respond with: Lord, you have the words of everlasting life.

Activity

Have students paste picture of Jesus on their ¼ piece of poster board. Print words: "Jesus is my Savior." (Explain Savior if necessary.) Have students decorate. Make available a selection of materials for students to choose from.

Letter to Parents

Dear Parents,

In your family prayer time, include a simple act of contrition and a prayer of thanksgiving to Jesus for being our Savior.

Sincerely in Christ,
Teacher _____

Questions

Who is Jesus' Father?

Do we call the church "God's house"?

Did Jesus die for us?

Did Jesus rise from the dead three days later?

Is Jesus our Savior?

Cycle B
Fourth Sunday of Lent

Jesus Is God's Gift to Us

Supplies Needed

One hemmed piece of material measuring approximately 8" × 11" or larger, per student. One inch hem at top. Use burlap, drapery material or other heavy cloth.

Dowel 10" long, one per student

String or yarn 12" long, one piece per student

Felt letters saying JESUS IS GOD'S GIFT TO ME, one set per student. (Pattern, page 71)

glue

Lesson

Jesus was talking to a friend named Nicodemus. He said, "God loved the world so much God gave his only son." [That son was Jesus.] Then Jesus said, "Whoever believes in me will not die but will have eternal life [live forever]."

Stress

Many times Jesus said things that were hard for people to understand. Do you know what eternal life means? (Live forever.) Where do we live forever? (In heaven with God.) When Jesus said, "Whoever believes in me will not die but will have eternal life," he was saying that although we may be dead to the other people here on earth, we will be alive to God in heaven.

Liturgy

Gather around altar. Join hands.

Sing "Thank You, God" from "Hi God," but change the wording to say: "Thank you, God, for giving us Jesus."

End liturgy by all saying: Let my tongue be silenced if I ever forget you.

Activity

Make banners that say: JESUS IS GOD'S GIFT TO ME.

So banners will be correct, have students place letters on material for approval before gluing. Place dowel in top hem. Tie string or yarn to each end of dowel for hanging.

Letter to Parents

Dear Parents,

Your child is bringing home a banner he/she made today. Jesus is the greatest gift we will ever receive. Include a prayer of thanksgiving in your family prayer time this week.

Sincerely in Christ,
Teacher _____

Questions

Will we live forever?

Where will we live forever?

Is Jesus God's greatest gift to us?

Cycle B
Fifth Sunday of Lent

Jesus Died So We Could All Come to Love God

Supplies Needed

stock of wheat

flower seeds

9" × 12" construction paper

potting soil (moistened)

pots or styrofoam cups (1 per student)

crayolas

picture of Jesus on cross (one per student)

PATTERN FOR BANNER
Number under letter indicates number required for each student.

Lesson

Jesus said to the people "Unless a grain of wheat falls to the ground and dies it remains [stays] a grain of wheat, but if it dies it produces much fruit." [Have a stock of wheat. Show the class one grain from the stock. Explain if that one grain is planted it will grow to be like the stock with many grains.] Jesus was talking about himself. He is like the grain of wheat. He had to die so many people could learn to love God.

Stress

Can anyone tell me why Jesus died? (To save us.) Or: Did Jesus die to save us?

People learned to love God because God sent Jesus to save us. If we love God, how do we show it? (By being good and by praying.)

Activity

Plant a seed. Have students fill small flower pots or styrofoam cups ¾ full with moist potting soil. Plant seed. (Nasturtiums are fast-growing.)

Liturgy

Gather around altar. Have crucifix on altar. Lay the stock of wheat on the altar. Join hands.

All:
Create a clean heart in me, O God.

Leader:
Jesus, you are like a grain of wheat.

All:
Create a clean heart in me, O God.

Leader:
Jesus, you died so we could all love God.

All:
Create a clean heart in me, O God.

All sing:
Tune: "Amazing Grace."
"Thank you, Jesus, thank you, Jesus, thank you, Jesus, thank you." (Repeat.)

Activity

Glue pictures of Jesus on the cross to a sheet of 9" × 12" construction paper. Have students draw wheat around crucifix. Use real wheat stock as model for drawing.

Letter to Parents

Dear Parents,
Your child is bringing home a seed he/she planted in class today. Help him/her to care for it. When the new plant appears, tell your child that Jesus is like the seed. Jesus died to bring new life to us, a new life in God.
Sincerely in Christ,
Teacher _____

Questions

Why did Jesus die?
(or) Did Jesus die to save us?
Should we love God?
How do we show our love for God?

PALM SUNDAY Cycles A-B-C all the same. See Palm Sunday—Cycle A for today's lesson.

SECOND SUNDAY OF EASTER Cycles A-B-C all the same. See Second Sunday of Easter—Cycle A for this lesson.

Cycle B
Third Sunday of Easter

Reverence for the Bible

Supplies Needed

1 candle per student	glue
sequins	glitter
beads	straight pins
soda straws (paper)	tissue paper
glass jar (2)	scissors

Activity

Bible enthronement. Teacher holds Bible and says: This is a Bible. The Bible tells us all about God. The Bible is sometimes called God's word or God's book. We handle the Bible with reverence.

(If students are familiar with the Bible, the teacher holds it and asks:)

What is this? [Bible.] What does the Bible tell us? (All about God.) The Bible is sometimes called _____ ? [God's word or God's book.] How do we handle the Bible? (With reverence.)

Today we are going to decorate the altar in a special way. Make artificial flowers and decorate two vases and candles.

Candles: Can be group activity or each student can decorate one. Use beads and sequins and pin into candles; or glue glitter or colored paper cut in flower or other designs. Give students a choice so the completed candles are their own creative work.

Flowers: Cut tissue paper into ovals. Twist to form bow (Fig. 1). Glue into bows to one end of soda straw (or pipe cleaner) at twisted point. Do not use plastic straws. Completed flowers look like sweet peas.

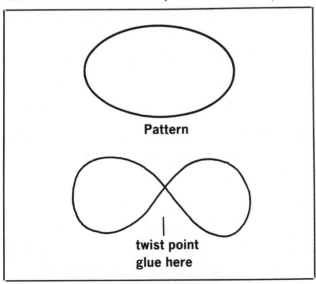

Pattern

twist point
glue here

Vases: Use any type of jar and decorate by gluing small torn pieces of tissue paper to jar. Cover completely. Overlapping paper gives added color effects. Have students work together on this project.

Lesson

Once again while all the disciples [Jesus' followers] were locked in the room, suddenly Jesus was there with them. He said, "Look at my hands and feet. Touch me. A ghost does not have flesh and bones as I do." The disciples were so happy. Jesus asked for some food. They gave him some cooked fish which he took and ate. [Ghosts do not eat.] Then he taught them the meaning of the scriptures. [The first part of the Bible tells us about God sending a redeemer, someone to save us so we can go to heaven. That redeemer is Jesus.]

Liturgy

Gather around altar. Sing: "Jesus Loves Me." (Words and gestures, 2nd Sunday of year—Cycle B)

All:
Let your face shine on us.

Give one another a greeting of peace. Be sure to greet each student.

Letter to Parents

Dear Parents,
   Today we discussed the Bible. What is it? We handle it reverently. Ask your child to tell you what he/she learned about the Bible today. Have the Bible present when you have your family prayer time.
                    Sincerely in Christ,
                    Teacher _____

Questions

What is the Bible? or
Is the Bible God's Word?
How do we treat the Bible?

Cycle B
Fourth Sunday of Easter

Jesus Is the Good Shepherd; We Are His Sheep

Supplies Needed

One sheet of poster board with a picture of Jesus the Good Shepherd pasted in the center.

Cutout of sheep (1 per student) cut of white construction paper or tag board. (See pattern, page 75.)

cotton balls

marking pens

glue

Lesson

A shepherd is a man who owns sheep. He leads his sheep to a pasture [a place where there is green grass for the sheep to eat]. The shepherd guards his sheep so nothing can hurt them as they eat. One day Jesus said, "I am the Good Shepherd. The Good Shepherd lays down his life for his sheep." [We are Jesus' sheep. Jesus died for us.] Jesus said, "I am the Good Shepherd. I know my sheep and my sheep know me in the same way that the Father knows me and I know the Father; for these sheep I will give my life."

[Jesus knows each one of us and is willing to die for us.]

Who is the Father Jesus is speaking of? [Or: Is it God the Father Jesus is speaking of?]

Activity

Poster of Jesus and sheep. Have one sheet of poster board with Jesus' picture on it. Give each student a cutout of a sheep. Students glue cotton balls, which have been pulled thin, onto sheep. Students glue completed sheep onto poster board. Each student then writes or prints his/her name under the sheep. Place completed poster on altar.

Liturgy

Gather around altar.

All:
The stone rejected by the builders has become the cornerstone.

Leader:
Jesus said, "I am the Good Shepherd."

All:
Jesus, I thank you.

Leader:
The Good Shepherd lays down his life for his sheep.

All:
Jesus, I thank you.

Leader:
Jesus said, "I am the Good Shepherd."

All:
Jesus, I thank you.

Leader:
'I know my sheep."

All:
Jesus, I thank you.

Leader:
"My sheep know me."

All:
Jesus, I thank you.

Leader:
"The same way the Father knows me and I know the Father."

All:
Jesus, I thank you.

Leader:
"For these sheep I will give my life."

All:
Jesus, I thank you. The stone rejected by the builders has become the cornerstone.

Letter to Parents

Dear Parents,
Today we heard the story of the Good Shepherd. In your family prayer time this week, use the following litany.
Sincerely in Christ,
Teacher _____

Note to Teacher

Include a copy of today's liturgy prayer in your letter to the parents.

Questions

Who is the Good Shepherd? or
Is Jesus the Good Shepherd?
Are we Jesus' sheep?
Does Jesus know us?

PATTERN FOR GOOD SHEPHERD POSTER

Have one cutout per student.
Cut of white construction paper or tag board.

Cycle B
Fifth Sunday of Easter

We Must Stay Close to Jesus
Let Jesus Be a Part of Us

Supplies Needed
copy of vine on page 77, one per student
pens or pencils

Activity
Go outside to a bush or vine. (Or bring a house plant to class.) Discuss what it needs to grow (earth, water, sun, etc.). Discuss its beauty and the beauty of the branches. All the branches get their nourishment of life through the vine. (Explain how the roots take up nourishment which travels through the main trunk to all the branches.) This is how the branches receive all they need to live. Cut off a small branch. Ask the students what is going to happen to the branch you cut off, and why. (It will die because it is no longer a part of the bush.) While still beside the bush, tell today's story.

Lesson
Jesus said, "I am the vine and you are the branches. If you live in me and my words stay part of you, you may ask what you will—it will be done for you."

Compare
As the branches of this bush get their life through the vine or main trunk, we get our life through Jesus. Jesus takes care of our needs as the vine takes care of the needs of the branches. Jesus wants us to stay close to him and ask him for what we need.

Activity
Give each student a picture of a vine. Have them print JESUS on the main branch, then add their name and the names of all their family members on the branches. (Pattern, page 77)

Liturgy
Gather around the altar. Join hands.

All:
I will praise you, Lord, in the assembly of your people.

Sing:
"Praise God"; tune: "Amazing Grace." (Repeat "Praise God" throughout entire song.)

End by all repeating above prayer.

Letter to Parents
Dear Parents,
This week we ask you and your child to perform an experiment. Place a leafy stalk of fresh celery in a juice glass which is ¾ full of water and 7 drops of red food coloring. Place it in the refrigerator. Tomorrow the celery should be changing color. Discuss with your child how the celery has drawn nourishment through the stalk to the leaves. This is what Jesus was telling us when he said, "I am the vine and you are the branches." We must stay close to Jesus for spiritual nourishment.
Sincerely in Christ,
Teacher _____

Questions
Are we like the branches on the vine?
Must we stay close to Jesus?
Does Jesus want us to ask him for everything we need?

Reproduce in green if possible. One per student.

Cycle B
Sixth Sunday of Easter

The Great Love God the Father and Jesus Have For Us and the Love We Must Give in Return

Supplies Needed
Two gift-wrapped boxes: one with a picture of Jesus as a man in it—box labeled "God's gift to us." The other with a picture of Jesus on the cross and a picture of Jesus resurrected—labeled: "Jesus' gift to us." Sheets of paper with words "I love Jesus; I will keep his commandments and love everyone."

pens
crayolas
glue
9" × 12" sheet construction paper, one per student
picture of Jesus on cross, greeting card size, one per student

Note to Teacher
As students arrive at class, teacher greets each with, "The love of Jesus be with you, _____."(Repeat at end of class.)

Lesson
Jesus said to his disciples: "As the father has loved me, so I have loved you." (Who is the Father that loves Jesus?)

Discuss
Ask the students: How much does God love us? (No answer they give is wrong for whatever they say God loves us at least that much and more.) Let a student open the gift from God. Inside is a picture of Jesus as a man. Teacher: God loves us so much he gave us his only son.

Ask the students: "How much does Jesus love us?" (Again, no answer they give is wrong for Jesus loves us even more.) Let a student open the gift from Jesus. Inside are two pictures, one of Jesus on the cross and one of the Resurrection. Teacher: Jesus loves us so much he died on the cross for us and rose from the dead.

Lesson (continued)
Jesus also said, "You will live in my love if you keep my commandments [laws]. This is my commandment. Love one another as I have loved you."

Activity
Have sheets of paper on which is printed, "I love Jesus. I will keep his commandments and love everyone." Have each student sign one. Be sure they know what it says before signing. When signed, place it on the altar. (Student may take it home after class.)

Liturgy
With pictures from gift boxes on altar, gather around and join hands.

All:
The Lord has revealed to the nations his saving power. Jesus, you died to save us. Jesus, I love you and thank you. To show my love I will keep your commandments [laws] and love everyone.

Give one another a greeting of peace by saying: "The love of Jesus be with you."

Activity
Glue pictures of Jesus on the cross onto 9" × 12" sheets of construction paper. Print "Jesus loves me" on each. (Student does own work, then decorates as he /she chooses.)

Letter to Parents
Dear Parents,
Today we learned of Jesus' great love for us. In your family prayer, include a greeting of peace by saying: "The love of Jesus be with you."

Sincerely in Christ,
Teacher _____
N.B. Parents are needed next week to provide transportation to a nursing home.

Questions

Who is the Father that loves Jesus? or
Is God the Father the one who loves Jesus?
Did God the Father love us enough to send us Jesus?
Does Jesus love us?
Does Jesus love us enough to die for us?
Do we love Jesus?
Do we show our love for Jesus by loving one another?

Cycle B
Seventh Sunday of Easter

We Pray with Jesus

Supplies Needed

Parents to transport students to nursing home. Make arrangements ahead with nursing home.

Hemmed material, approximately 8" × 11" or 9" × 12". Top hem 1" deep. One per student. Use colored burlap, drapery samples or other heavy material.

One 10" dowel per student

One piece of string of yarn

12" long, per student

One set of letters cut of felt or other heavy material, per student. (See pattern, page 81.)

Note to Teacher

Greet each student as they arrive by saying, "The love of Jesus be with you, _____."

Explain: One day shortly before he died for us Jesus prayed for his apostles. We are going to join Jesus in that prayer today.

Gather around altar. Sit on chairs in a semicircle. Feet flat on floor. Hands in lap in open prayer position. Eyes closed.

(A teacher's aide reads the parts of Jesus' prayer. The teacher gives an explanation. Students respond with the responsorial psalm.)

Reader:
O father most holy,
Protect them with your name.

Teacher:
God, our father in heaven, is holy. He will protect us from sin if we ask him.

All:
The Lord has set his throne in heaven.

Reader:
That they may be one even as we are one.

Teacher:
Jesus wants us to be as one in our love for him and others. Jesus and God the Father are one, especially in their love for each other and us.

All:
The Lord has set his throne in heaven.

Reader:
As long as I was with them, I guarded them with your name.

Teacher:
Jesus cared for his apostles. Jesus cares for us.

All:
The Lord has set his throne in heaven.

Reader:
I kept careful watch, and not one of them was lost.

Teacher:
If we trust in Jesus we will not loose him.

All:
The Lord has set his throne in heaven.

Reader:
Now I come to you: I say this while I am still in the world that they may share my joy completely.

Teacher:
Jesus would soon die and return to his father in heaven. He wanted the apostles to be happy for him.

All:
The Lord has set his throne in heaven.

Reader:
I do not ask you to take them out of the world, but to guard them from the evil one.

Teacher:
Jesus was not asking God to take his apostles with him. He asked God to keep them safe from the devil. Jesus wants us to be safe from the devil.

All:
The Lord has set his throne in heaven.

Reader:
As you have sent me into the world, so I have sent them into the world.

Teacher:
God had sent Jesus to teach everyone about God. Now Jesus was sending the apostles to teach others about God also.

All:
The Lord has set his throne in heaven.

Activity
Jesus wants us to tell others about God. Make banners for the shut-ins at a nearby nursing home. (Make arrangements ahead of time so the home will be prepared to receive you and the students.) Banner reads: God loves you. Have students place letters on banner in proper order before gluing to assure they are correct. After gluing letters in place, put dowel in top hem and attach cord for hanging. Cord can be either string or yarn. (See pattern for letters, page 81.)

Letter to Parents
Dear Parents,
   Today we prayed with Jesus and visited our nursing home friends. Jesus wants us to

be safe from all evil. This week in your family prayer, ask Jesus to protect everyone, especially spiritually.

Sincerely in Christ,
Teacher _____

Questions
Did Jesus pray?
Can we pray with Jesus?
Mass is another time we pray with Jesus.

PENTECOST SUNDAY same as Cycle A—See page 31.
TRINITY SUNDAY same as Cycle A—See page 32.

Cycle B
Twenty-third Sunday of Year

We Appreciate the Gifts of Hearing and Speech

Supplies Needed
record (anyone the students will like.)
cotton balls, 2 per student
adhesive tape cut in 2″ strips, 2 per student

Activity
Give students two pieces of adhesive tape. Have them tape their mouths shut. With their mouths taped, have each of the students try to tell the others something that happened to them the day before. Play a record the students like; part way through it, have the students put cotton in their ears and cover their ears with their hands.

Discuss how it feels to be unable to hear or talk.

Lesson
Some people brought Jesus a deaf man [someone who cannot hear] who also had a

LETTER PATTERNS FOR BANNER
Number under letters indicates number required for each student.

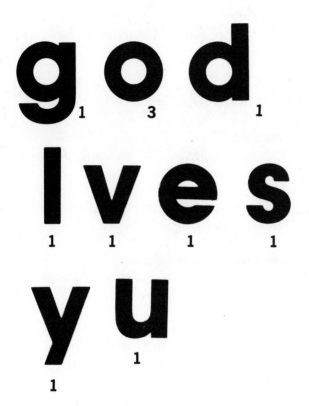

g o d
1 3 1

l v e s
1 1 1 1

y u
1
1

speech impediment [could not talk plainly]. They asked Jesus to cure him [make him well].

Jesus put his fingers in the man's ears and touched the man's tongue. Then he looked up to heaven and said, "Be opened." At once the man could hear and speak plainly. Everyone was amazed and said, "He makes the deaf hear and the mute speak."

Liturgy
Gather around altar. Join hands.

All:
O Lord, thank you for the gift of hearing. Praise the Lord, my soul. O Lord, thank you for the gift of speaking. Praise the Lord, my soul.

Sing:
"Praise God"; tune: "Amazing Grace." Repeat "Praise God" throughout entire song.

Letter to Parents
Dear Parents,
In your family prayer this week, include a prayer of thanks for the gifts of hearing and speaking.

Sincerely in Christ,
Teacher _____

Questions
Should we thank God for being able to talk?
Should we thank God for being able to hear?

Cycle B
Twenty-fourth Sunday of Year

Jesus Died and Rose Again to Save Us

Supplies Needed
2 twigs per student (1 approximately 6" long;
1 approximately 8" long)
1 paper-covered wire twist tie per student
1 short pipe cleaner per student
1 6" square of tissue paper per student

Lesson
Jesus asked his disciples [his followers], "Who do people say I am?" They told Jesus, "Some say John the Baptizer, others say one of the prophets" [A holy man].

Jesus asked, "Who do you say I am?"

Peter said, "You are the messiah" [the redeemer or the one who has come to save us].

Then Jesus began to tell his disciples that he would have to suffer and be put to death, but he would rise again in three days.

Discuss
How do you think the disciples felt when Jesus told them he was to die? (Encourage students to express their feelings.)

Jesus also said he would rise again. In Mass tomorrow we will say this prayer: "I will walk in the presence of the Lord in the land of the living."

That means, when we die we will rise again and live with God.

Liturgy
Gather around altar. Join hands.

All:
I will walk in the presence of the Lord in the land of the living.

Leader:
Thank you, Jesus, for dying to save us.

All:
I will walk in the presence of the Lord in the land of the living.

Leader:
Thank you, Jesus, for rising from the dead.

All:
I will walk in the presence of the Lord in the land of the living.

Leader:
Thank you, Jesus, for preparing a place in heaven for me.

All:
I will walk in the presence of the Lord in the land of the living.

Activity
Make a cross of twigs. Form cross of twigs and fasten with paper-covered wire twist tie. Make a flower to fasten to cross. Pinch center of tissue paper square and twist. Attach pipe cleaner to twisted portion (Fig. 1). Fasten to cross.

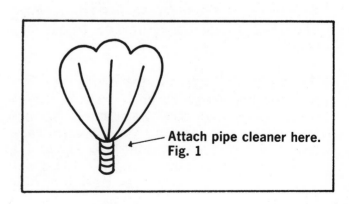

Attach pipe cleaner here.
Fig. 1

Letter to Parents

Questions

Is Jesus our Savior?
Did Jesus die for us?
Did Jesus rise from the dead?

Cycle B
Twenty-fifth Sunday of Year

We Serve Others

Supplies Needed

strip of brown wrapping paper
scissors
glue
magazines
pictures of children
broad-tipped marking pen

Note to Teacher

Do not prepare the classroom ahead of time today. Have students set up prayer altar and class work area. Give each student a task to perform.

Lesson

The twelve apostles [Jesus' closest disciples or followers] were arguing who was the most important. Jesus told them, "If anyone wishes to be first [most important] he must remain last [be less important] and a servant [one who waits on others] to all." [As we did today, each of us served all the others by helping to prepare our classroom.].

Jesus took a little child and putting his arms around him, said to them, "Whoever welcomes a child such as this for my sake welcomes me. And whoever welcomes me welcomes, not me, but him who sent me." [God, our father, sent Jesus to us.]

Liturgy

Gather around altar. Join hands.

Sing:

"Jesus Loves Me." (Words and gestures, Second Sunday of Year—Cycle B.)

All:

The Lord upholds my Life.
I will serve others.
The Lord upholds my life.

Activity

Make a mural.

On a strip of brown wrapping paper, have students glue pictures of children cut or torn from magazines. (Old mission calendars often have pictures of children of foreign lands.) When complete, with a broad-tipped marking pen, print: WELCOME CHILDREN. Give the mural to the pre-school teacher or first grade teacher for his/her classroom.

Letter to Parents

Questions

What did Jesus tell us to do if we want to be first with him?
Do we serve others cheerfully?

Cycle B
Twenty-sixth Sunday of Year

Everyone Belongs to Jesus

Supplies Needed
Parents to transport class to nursing home.

Liturgy
Gather around altar. Join hands.

Leader:
In your name, O Lord, we will give to others.

All:
The precepts [laws] of the Lord give joy to the heart.

Leader:
Because everyone belongs to you, we will give to others.

All:
The precepts of the Lord give joy to the heart.

Lesson
John [one of the apostles] said to Jesus, "Teacher, we saw a man using your name to drive the devil out of people and we tried to stop him because he was not one of us."

Jesus said, "Do not try to stop him. No man who performs a miracle using my name can speak ill [badly] of me. Any man who gives you a drink of water because you belong to Christ will not go without his reward."

Discuss
Everyone belongs to Christ. Today we are going to visit a nursing home. All the elderly people there belong to Christ. We will take them our gifts of cookies.

(Make arrangements ahead of time with the nursing home. Have them select which patients the students will visit, preferably someone who has very little or no company. Each student should adopt one of the elderly as his/her special friend.)

Letter to Parents
Dear Parents,

This week we visited a nursing home and each student adopted one of the patients. Your child's special friend is [patient's name]. Please include a prayer for him/her in your family prayer time this week.

Sincerely in Christ,
Teacher _____

Questions
Does everyone belong to Jesus?
Do we give to others because they belong to Jesus?
Are we kind to others because they belong to Jesus?
Do we love others because they belong to Jesus?

Cycle B
Twenty-seventh Sunday of Year

Supplies Needed
11 oz. soup can per student
felt piece 4" × 8½" per student
toilet tissue core per student
felt piece 4½" × 5½" per student
two sets of felt letters per student
(use contrasting color to larger pieces)
glue

Lesson
Some pharisees [leaders of the people] to test Jesus asked him, "Is it all right for a man to divorce his wife?"

Jesus said, "Let no man separate what God has joined."

Discuss
Sometimes it is hard to get along with people we live with, even though we love them. They do not always understand us. We do not always understand them. Even married peo-

ple who love each other very much have problems. Today we are going to pray for our parents and all the married people we know.

Liturgy
Gather around altar. Join hands.

All:
May the Lord bless us all the days of our lives. Bless especially our mothers and fathers. Bless also [here let students name some married relatives and/or friends. End with:] May the Lord bless us all the days of our lives.

Activity
Make a gift for students' parents.

Suggestions:

1. Cover a clean 11 oz. soup can with felt. Decorate with word LOVE cut of contrasting felt. Use as pencil holder for Dad.

2. Cover a toilet tissue core with felt. Decorate with word LOVE cut of contrasting felt. Use as holder for electric appliance cords for Mother.

Letter to Parents
Dear Parents,
   Today your child is bringing home an expression of his/her love for you. One is a pencil holder for Father; the other an electric appliance cord holder for Mother.
                    Sincerely in Christ,
                    Teacher _____

Questions
Do parents sometimes have problems?
Should we pray every day for our parents?

Cycle B
Twenty-eighth Sunday of Year

We Are Willing to Give Everything to Jesus Jesus Comes First

Supplies Needed
large ash tray
slips of lined paper
pencils
lined stationery
construction paper
crayolas
envelopes (1 per student)
postage stamps (1 per student)

Lesson
One day a man came running up to Jesus and said, "Good teacher, what must I do to share an everlasting life?" [Live forever in heaven].

Jesus said, "Obey the commandments" [God's laws]. The man said, "Teacher, I have kept all these since my childhood."

Jesus looked at him with love and told him, "There is one thing more you must do. Go and sell what you have and give it to the poor; you will have treasure in heaven. After that come and follow me."

The man went away sad for he was very rich.

Discuss
Tell me something you have that you love very much. [Have each child name some possession. Have them write it on a piece of paper.]

Could you give it to Jesus? If they say "yes," have them place their slip of paper in a large ashtray on the altar.

Liturgy
Gather around altar.

Ask the students to quietly offer their favorite possession to Jesus. Sit quiet for a few minutes. Light the slips of paper. When they have burned, all say: Fill us with your love, O Lord, and we will sing for joy.

Sing:
One verse of "Joy, Joy, Joy," from "Hi God."

Activity
Write a note or draw a picture for our new friends at the nursing home. (Mail them after class.)

Letter to Parents
Dear Parents,
Encourage your child to share his/her possessions with the family and friends this week. We learned in class today that we must be willing to give up everything for Jesus.
Sincerely in Christ,
Teacher _____

Questions
Should we be willing to give up everything for Jesus?
If we do, would Jesus be first in our lives?

To Be Great We Must Serve the Needs of Others

Supplies needed
package of moist towelettes
graham crackers
juice
pens
paper cups
paper napkins
slips of paper with words: I will set the table for the family meal every day this week.

Activity
Have a package of moist towelettes. Divide class into partners. One partner gently washes the face of the other; when finished, change roles. When the students have had their faces washed, ask them to tell how it felt to have their faces washed. Ask the students to tell how it felt to wash one another's face.

Lesson
Jesus called the apostles [his special friends] together and said. "Anyone among you who wants to be great must serve [wait on] the rest. Whoever wants to be first among you must serve the needs of all."

Activity
Have a small party of graham crackers and juice. Divide the work of preparing the table and serving so each student has a task to perform. While enjoying the snack, talk about how students felt while doing their part in the preparation. Discuss the possibility of serving the family at home by setting the table for the family meal every day this week. Give each student a slip of paper that says, "I will set the table for the family meal every day this week." Have each sign the slip of paper.

Liturgy

Gather around altar. Place the slips of paper just signed on the altar.

Prayer: Lord, let your mercy be on us as we place our trust in you. Jesus, teach me to be great by serving others. Lord, let your mercy be on us as we place our trust in you.

(Let students take signed slips home.)

Letter to Parents

Dear Parents,

Jesus tells us that to be great we must serve the needs of others. Encourage your child to serve others by setting the table for the family meal every day this week.

Sincerely in Christ,
Teacher _____

Questions

To be great must we serve others?
How can we serve others every day?

Cycle B
Thirtieth Sunday of Year

We Appreciate the Gift of Sight

Supplies Needed

blindfolds (1 per student)
sack of objects for students to identify
(1 object per student)

Activity

Blindfold students. Give each an object to identify by feeling, smelling, tasting and listening. Then have students walk to you one at a time by following your directions and the sound of your voice. Remove blindfolds and discuss how it felt to be unable to see.

Lesson

As Jesus was leaving the town of Jericho with his disciples and a large crowd, there was a blind beggar named Bartimaeus sitting by the roadside. On hearing Jesus was coming he called out, "Jesus, have pity on me." People were scolding him to make him keep quiet but he shouted all the louder, "Jesus, have pity on me." Jesus said, "Be on your way your faith [trust that Jesus could cure him] has healed you." Immediately he received his sight and started to follow Jesus.

Discuss

How do you think Bartimaeus felt when Jesus cured him?

Liturgy

Gather around the altar.

All:

The Lord has done great things for us; we are filled with joy. Lord, thank you for letting me see. [Have students each name something they are happy to see.] The Lord has done great things for us; we are filled with joy.

Sing:

"Joy, Joy, Joy" from "Hi God" (one verse).

Letter to Parents

Dear Parents,

In your family prayers this week, include a prayer of thanks for the gift of sight.

Sincerely in Christ,
Teacher _____

Questions

Are we happy we can see?
Should we thank God for letting us see?
Does God give us many beautiful things to see?

Cycle B
Thirty-first Sunday of Year

The Greatest Commandment, "Love God"

Supplies Needed
burlap or drapery sample (one per student) approximately 5″ × 7″ hemmed. Top hem 1″ deep.
one dowel per student 6″ long
one piece string or yarn per student, 7″ long
one set letters per student (cut of felt). See pattern, this page.
glue

Lesson
One day a man asked Jesus "Which is the first of all the commandments?" [laws].

Jesus said, "Love the Lord your God with all your heart, with all your soul, with all your mind and with all your strength. The second commandment is you shall love your neighbor as yourself. There is no other commandment greater than these."

Liturgy
Gather around altar. Join hands.

All:
I love you, Lord, my strength.

Sing:
"Love God" to tune "Amazing Grace." Repeat words "Love God" throughout song.

All:
I love you, Lord, my strength.

Activity
Make banner. Love God.

Have students place letters before gluing so you can check for accuracy.

BANNER PATTERN

LOVE
1   2   1   1

GD
1   1

Number under letter indicates number needed per student.

Letter to Parents

Dear Parents,

Today we learned the two great commandments, love God and love our neighbor as ourself. In your prayers this week, tell God you love him. It is good to say aloud, "Dear God, I love you."

Sincerely in Christ,
Teacher _____

N.B. Have your child wear old clothes next week.

Questions

Is the greatest commandment to love God? Must we also love others as we love ourselves?

Cycle B
Thirty-second Sunday of Year

We Love and Praise God

Supplies Needed

butcher paper, one piece 9" × 12" or larger per student
oil cloth or newspaper to protect work area
liquid starch
dry tempra paint
To make finger paint: pour ⅛ C liquid starch on butcher paper; sprinkle on dry tempra paint; paint mixes as student begins to work.
small box
circles, size of a quarter, cut of tag board, write 1¢ on each circle (approximately 50)

Activity

Give the students tag board coins. To a couple of students, give *only two,* but give several to the rest of the class. Have a small box. One at a time, ask the students with the most coins to put several but not all in the box. End with the students who have only two coins; ask these to put both coins in the box. As each student places coins in the box, ask if it was hard to give up the coins and why or why not.

Lesson

Jesus watched the people putting money in the collection box. Many rich people put in large amounts but one poor widow [a lady whose husband is dead] came and put in two small coins worth about a cent. Jesus said to his disciples, "This poor widow gave more than the rich men. They gave from their surplus [large amount of money] but she gave all she has to live on."

Discuss

Last week we learned the greatest law is to love God. Did this woman love God? A few weeks ago we said we were willing to give our favorite possession to God. The woman in today's story gave everything she had.

Liturgy

Gather around altar. Join hands. Raise joined hands high. Together *shout:* Praise the Lord, my soul.

Sing:

"Praise God"—tune "Amazing Grace" (repeat, "Praise God" throughout song.)

All say:

Praise God, my soul.

Activity

Finger-paint, "Praise God." Use heavy butcher paper (thin paper bleeds). Use one color. Finger-paint the entire sheet, then have students finger-print or write "Praise God" on their work.

Letter to Parents

Dear Parents,

Use prayers of love and praise to God in your family prayer time this week. Include the psalm: "Praise the Lord, My soul."

Sincerely in Christ,
Teacher _____

Questions

Do we love God?
Should we praise God?

Cycle B
Thirty-third Sunday of Year

We Prepare for, and Thank Jesus for, His Second Coming

Supplies Needed
¼ poster board per student (use any color except white or yellow)
Cutout of chalice, one per student (use yellow construction paper); pattern, page 91
Cutout of host, one per student (use white construction paper); pattern, page 91
yellow yarn, one piece 36″ long per student
white yarn, one piece 13″ long per student
other colored yarn in small pieces
glue
pencils

Lesson
Jesus said to his disciples; "After many trials [problems] of every sort the sun will be darkened, the moon will not shed its light, stars will fall out of the skies and the heavens will shake. Then men will see the son of man [Jesus] coming in the clouds with great power and glory. He will send his messengers [ones who run errands] to gather his chosen ones from all over. As to the exact day or hour, all this will happen, no one knows, only God the Father.

Discuss
Someday Jesus will come back for us. We don't know when that will be. We must always be ready to meet Jesus.

Liturgy
Gather around altar. Join hands.

All:
Keep me safe, O God, you are my hope.
Thank you, Jesus, for loving me.
Thank you, Jesus, for the day you will come back for me.
Keep me safe, O God, for you are my hope.

Activity
Have students glue chalice and host on poster board. With white yarn, outline host. With yellow yarn, outline chalice. Write or print in pencil: Come, Lord Jesus. Glue yarn over words.

Letter to Parents
Dear Parents,
   As Thanksgiving approaches, keep prayers of thanks for God's many blessings in your family prayer time.

Sincerely in Christ,
Teacher _____

Questions
Should we thank Jesus because he is coming again someday?
Should we always be ready to meet Jesus?

Cycle B
Thirty-fourth Sunday of Year

Jesus Is Christ the King

Supplies Needed
¼ poster board per student
greeting card size picture of Jesus as an adult, one per student
cutouts of hearts, any size
cutouts of crowns, any size
glue
crayolas

Lesson
Pilate said, "So, then, you are a king?" Jesus said, "It is you who say I am a king. The reason I came into the world, is to testify [tell] to the truth. Anyone committed [promised] to the truth hears my voice."

Discuss
Jesus is Christ the King of heaven and earth. A king is a ruler. Jesus rules the whole world. Jesus is King of our hearts. We hear Jesus' voice.

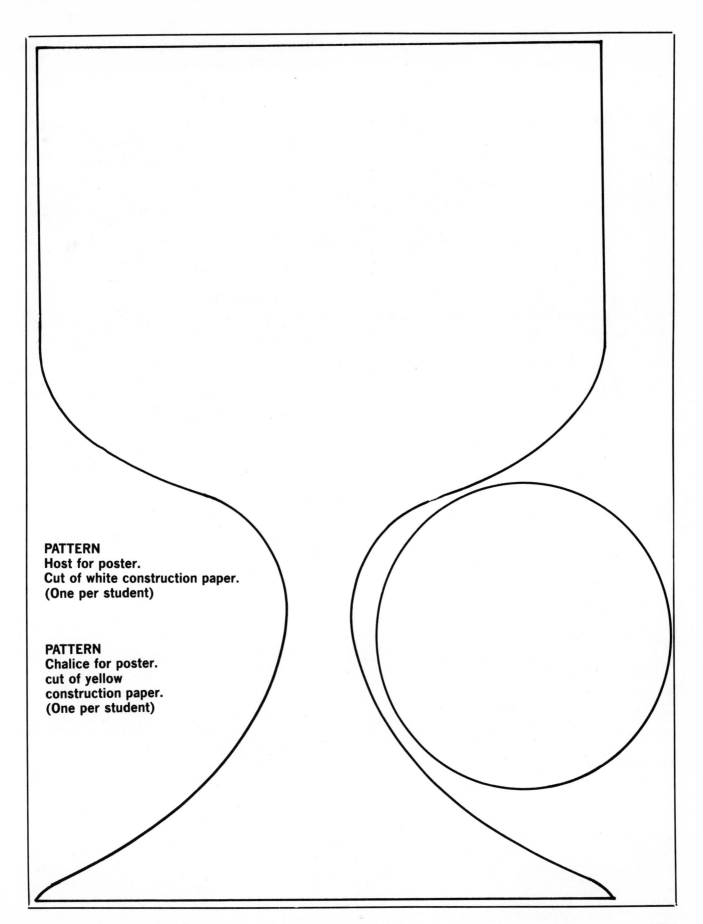

PATTERN
Host for poster.
Cut of white construction paper.
(One per student)

PATTERN
Chalice for poster.
cut of yellow
construction paper.
(One per student)

Liturgy
Gather around altar.

All:
The Lord is king, he is robed in majesty.

Song:
"The King of Glory" from "Songs of Good News" or "To Jesus Christ, Our Sovereign King."

All:
The Lord is king, he is robed in majesty.

Activity
Make a collage of "Jesus, King of my heart." Use picture of Jesus, as an adult; heart cutouts; and crown cutouts. Add words: Jesus, king of my heart.

Letter to Parents
Dear Parents,

Jesus is Christ the King, ruler of our hearts. In your family prayers this week, invite Jesus into your hearts to reign as King and ruler of your lives.

Sincerely in Christ,
Teacher _____

Questions
Is Jesus Christ the King?
Does Jesus rule our hearts?

Note to Teacher
Next week, go to the First Sunday of Advent—Cycle C.

CYCLE C

Cycle C
First Sunday of Advent

Be Ready to Meet Jesus

Supplies Needed
Ruled 12" × 18" sheets of construction paper, one per student. (See pattern, page 94 and instructions, this page.)
felt marking pens (purple)
Candle cutouts, one set per student (See pattern, page 95.)
One set letters per student (pattern, page 95.)
Advent wreath (See instructions to make, page 4.)

Lesson
Jesus said many things that were hard to understand. One day he said to his disciples [followers], "There will be signs in the sun, the moon and the stars. On earth nations will be upset at the roaring of the sea and the waves. Men will die of fright because they won't know what is happening. After that you will see the son of man [Jesus] coming on a cloud with great power and glory. Stand up straight, raise your heads, for ransom [reward] is near. [Jesus was telling everyone to always be ready to meet him, no matter what happens, and we will be all right].

Liturgy
Gather around altar. Light one candle on the Advent wreath. Stand up straight, raise your heads as Jesus said. With hands raised high, say:

All:
To you, O Lord, I lift my soul. Come, Lord Jesus, we are waiting for you. To you, O Lord, I lift my soul.

Activity
Make Advent calendars, (See pattern, page 94, and instructions, this page.)

Letter to Parents
Dear Parents,
Again this year, assemble your Advent wreath for use at the family meal or family prayer time.
We are preparing to meet Jesus by doing something special each day for someone else. Encourage your child in this. At the end of each day, if your child has succeeded, he/she is to add either a candle or a letter to the day's date on the Advent calendar.
Sincerely in Christ,
Teacher _____

Questions
Is Jesus coming again?
Should we always be ready to meet him?

Advent Calendar Instructions
Using Fig. 1, page 94, prepare in advance one for each student. Draw all lines with purple felt-tip pen. Pencil in lightly month, days and numbers for any students who need a guide to follow. Let all other students do their own.

If the first Sunday of Advent falls in November, print the month as shown in the first two squares of Fig. 1. Have students enter dates in upper right-hand corner of each square, only to December 25.

PATTERN FOR ADVENT CALENDAR:

18"

DECEMBER

	SUNDAY	MONDAY	TUESDAY	WEDNESDAY	THURSDAY	FRIDAY	SATURDAY
	NOV. 29	NOV. 30					

2"

2¹/₂"

12"

Fig. 1.

94

Explain

We spend Advent preparing for the coming of Jesus at Christmas. We spend our lives preparing to meet Jesus by doing good. Each day we will try to do something special for someone else, then add a sticker to our calendar.

Each week, give students an envelope of stickers:
1st week: COME and 3 candles
2nd week: LORD and 3 candles
3rd week: JESUS and 2 candles
4th week: Enough stars to cover dates to 25th.

One Way to Prepare to Meet Jesus Is: Be Sorry For Your Sins

Supplies Needed

Advent wreath	glue
construction paper	crayolas
old Christmas cards	marking pens
scissors	calendar
second week's stickers for Advent	

LETTER PATTERNS

Cut one set per student. Use gummed colored paper or flocked adhesive shelf paper.

COME
LORD
JESUS

Candle: Fig. 2.
Cut 8 per student.
Use colored sticky paper,
available in stationery stores,
or use flocked adhesive shelf paper.

Activity

Talk about the Advent calendar from last week. Let students tell some of the things they did.

Lesson

John, the son of Zechariah [we know him as John the Baptist], was preaching by the River Jordan telling the people to repent [be sorry for their sins]. Many people did repent and were baptized in the river.

Liturgy

Gather around altar. Light two candles on the Advent wreath. Join hands, bow heads, close eyes. Quietly teacher says: Let us think about any wrong we have done and tell God we are sorry. Short pause, then say together:

All:

Dear God, I am sorry for all my faults. Please, forgive me. [Pause.] The Lord has done great things for us; we are filled with joy.

Sing:

"Joy, Joy, Joy" from "Hi God."

Activity

Make a greeting card to send to someone we have wronged or to some one who is lonely. Use colored construction paper, 9" × 12", folded in half. Paste picture from old Christmas card on front; write own message inside. Help those who need it with their message.

Be sure old cards used depict the true meaning of Christmas. Avoid secular cards, pictures of the flight into Egypt and shepherds seeing the star (the Magi followed the star, *not* the shepherds).

Letter to Parents

Dear Parents,

Our theme this week was repentance. In your family prayer, include a prayer of contrition. Our prayer today was "Dear God, I am sorry for all my faults. Please, forgive me."

Encourage your child to continue the Advent calendar. This week's word is "Lord."

Light two candles on your Advent wreath this week.

> *Sincerely in Christ,*
> *Teacher _____*

Question

Is being sorry for our wrongs or sins one way to prepare to meet Jesus?
Should we tell God we are sorry?

Cycle C
Third Sunday of Advent

Be Concerned About Others

Supplies Needed

Advent wreath
tokens (marked 1¢)
cookies or graham crackers (one per student)
(Use graham crackers instead of cookies if any students are diabetic or hyperkinetic.)
Stickers for third week of Advent
Matching cards (see Activity, page 97), one set per student

Activity

Give each student tokens with 1¢ on them. Do *not* divide them evenly. Have just enough cookies on hand so there is one for each student. Sell the cookies to the students for five tokens. Some will have just enough tokens; some will have more than enough; and others less than enough. See if the students will share without your having to tell them to do so. It may be necessary to point out, "[Name] doesn't have enough tokens."

Lesson

Last week we heard how John the Baptist told people to repent [be sorry for wrongs done and start to be good.]

Many people came to John and asked, "What should we do?" John said, "Let the man who has two coats give one to the man with none. The man who has food should do the same." [He was telling them to share. Compare to opening activity.] To other people he said, "Be honest." To other people he said, "Do not bully anyone [Be kind]. Do not tell lies [Be truthful]. Be happy with what you have" [Be satisfied].

Discuss
John told the people to be honest; to be kind; to be truthful; to share and be satisfied. Do you think he would tell us the same things if he were here today?

Activity
Matching cards:
Be kind
Be satisfied
Share
Be truthful
Be honest

Liturgy
Gather around altar. Light three candles on the Advent wreath.

All:
Cry out with joy and gladness: for among you is the great and holy one of Israel.

Teacher:
Jesus is the great and holy one of Israel. He is coming on Christmas Day. Let us say: "Come, Lord Jesus. Come into my heart. For you I will be kind, truthful, honest, satisfied, and share what I have."

Sing:
A Christmas carol the students select.

Letter to Parents,
Dear Parents,
   Today our gospel story told us to be kind, truthful, satisfied, honest, and to share. You can strengthen these virtues in your child by a word of praise each time he/she displays one.
   The word on our Advent calendar for this week is "Jesus."

Sincerely in Christ,
Teacher _____

Questions
Should we share with others?
Should we be kind?
Should we always tell the truth?
Should we be honest?
Should we be satisfied with what we have?

Cycle C
Fourth Sunday of Advent

We Help Others Willingly and Cheerfully

Supplies Needed
stickers for fourth week of Advent calendar
magazines
scissors
glue
poster board, one sheet

Lesson
Mary set out, hurrying into the hill country to a town of Judah where she entered Zechariah's house and greeted Elizabeth. Elizabeth said, "Blessed are you among women and blessed is the fruit of your womb."

Discuss
Mary knew Elizabeth needed her help. Mary went willingly to see Elizabeth and help her. Elizabeth had not asked Mary to help, but Mary offered to help for she knew Elizabeth needed her help.

When someone asks us to help, do we always help them? Do we help them willingly and cheerfully? Do we always wait until we are asked before we help? Do we sometimes offer to help before we are asked?

Activity
Make a collage of people helping others.

Liturgy
Gather around altar.

All:
Lord, make us turn to you; let us see your face and we shall be saved.

Say the Hail Mary with gestures:
HAIL MARY (right hand raised as if to wave)
FULL OF GRACE (arms crossed on chest)
THE LORD (arms raised heavenward)
IS WITH YOU. (hands extended straight ahead)
BLESSED ARE YOU (arms crossed on chest)
AMONG WOMEN (arms spread wide)
AND BLESSED IS THE FRUIT OF YOUR WOMB, (arms crossed on chest)
JESUS. (with arms still crossed, bow head)
HOLY MARY, (arms still crossed, raise head)
MOTHER OF GOD, (raise arms heavenward)
PRAY FOR US SINNERS (strike breast with right hand)
NOW AND AT THE HOUR OF OUR DEATH, AMEN. (hands folded and head bowed)

Letter to Parents
Dear Parents,
Today we heard the story of the Visitation of Mary to Elizabeth. We discussed Mary's willingness to help. Encourage your child's helpfulness by words of praise.
Light all four candles of the Advent wreath.
May the blessings of Christmas be yours,
Teacher_____

Questions
Did Mary help Elizabeth willingly and cheerfully?
Should we help others willingly and cheerfully?
Did Mary wait to be asked before helping?
Should we always wait to be asked before helping?

FIRST SUNDAY OF YEAR—CYCLE C

See First Sunday of Year—Cycle B, page 52

Cycle C
Second Sunday of Year

Begin to Build the Concept of a Miracle
Be Able to See a Need and Assist Before Being Asked

Supplies Needed
frozen grape juice concentrate or other grape drink
pitcher
glasses
water
tablespoon

Activity
Have students prepare grape juice or grape drink. Discuss what they had to do to prepare the grape drink. Drink the juice.

Lesson
There was a wedding in the town of Cana. Jesus, his mother and disciples [followers] were all invited to the celebration [party]. They ran out of wine. Jesus' mother told him, "They have no more wine." Jesus said, "Woman, how does this involve me?" His mother told those waiting on table. "Do whatever he tells you."

"Fill the jars with water," Jesus ordered. They filled them to the top. "Now," he said, "Draw some out and take it to the waiter in charge." They did as he told them. The waiter in charge tasted the water made wine and said to the groom, "People usually serve the best wine first and the lesser [poorer] wine last but you have kept the finest wine until now." This was Jesus' first miracle.

Discuss

What did Jesus do to change the water into wine? (Compare to the preparation of the grape juice at the beginning of class.) Did Jesus' mother ask Jesus to change the water into wine? (No, she just pointed out the need.) Does mother have to ask us each time she wants us to do something? Do we sometimes offer to help without being asked? Name something you can offer to do at home. (Set table; dust; vacuum, etc.)

Teach song on this page.

Liturgy

Gather around altar. Join hands.

All:
Proclaim his marvelous deeds to all the nations.

Teacher:
What marvelous deed did Jesus do today?

All:
Sing song just learned.

Tune: "When Johnny Comes Marching Home."

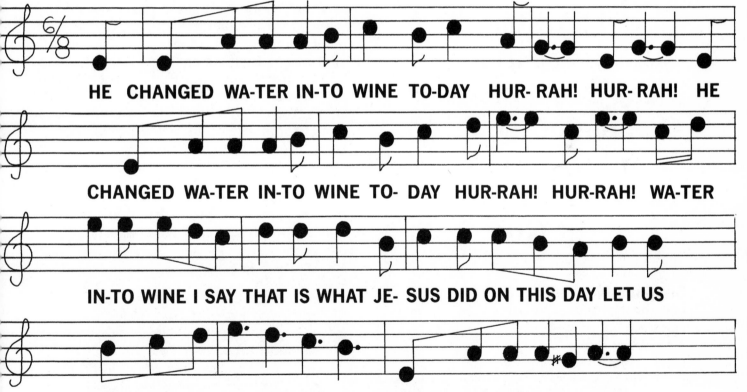

HE CHANGED WA-TER IN-TO WINE TO-DAY HUR-RAH! HUR-RAH! HE

CHANGED WA-TER IN-TO WINE TO-DAY HUR-RAH! HUR-RAH! WA-TER

IN-TO WINE I SAY THAT IS WHAT JE-SUS DID ON THIS DAY LET US

SING AND ALL BE GAY FOR HE CHANGED WA-TER IN-TO WINE.

Letter to Parents.

Dear Parents,

Today we encouraged the students to do their regular chores at home without waiting to be told. Ask your child to tell you what Jesus did today. Hopefully your answer will be sung to you. We heard the story of the wedding at Cana and learned a song about Jesus changing water into wine.

Sincerely in Christ,
Teacher _____

Questions

Do you have regular chores to do at home?
Do you wait to be told before you do them?

Cycle C
Third Sunday of Year

Old Testament Prepared the People for the Coming of the Savior, Jesus
The Bible Is the Word of God

Supplies Needed

one sheet of poster board
scissors
pictures of Bible
glue
felt pens

Lesson

One day Jesus returned to the town of Nazareth where he had grown up. He entered the synagogue [church] and stood up to do the reading. Jesus read: "The spirit of the Lord is upon me, for he has anointed me. He sent me to bring good news to the poor and re-covery of sight to the blind." Jesus sat down. When everyone was looking at him he said, "Today this scripture passage is fulfilled in your hearing."

[Jesus was telling the people: What I have just read was written about me. I am the one God's spirit is upon. I am God's anointed one. I have come to bring the good news to the poor and give sight to the blind.]

Activity

Take Bible and explain it is divided into two parts. The first part, called the Old Testament, is all they had when Jesus lived because it is the part that was written to help the people to prepare for the Savior's coming into the world. Jesus was that Savior. He told the people that day when he finished reading.

Have the students make a poster about the Bible. Let it be their creative effort. Suggestions: Draw a picture of the Bible or use pictures of Bibles from old Christmas and Easter greeting cards. Have students suggest words to print on the poster (i.e., Bible, God's Word, God's Book, etc.). Add Sunday's responsorial psalm to poster: Your words, Lord, are spirit and life.

Liturgy

Place completed poster on altar with Bible. Read together the psalm from poster. Sing: "The Spirit of the Lord" (see page 101.)

Letter to Parents

Dear Parents,

Talk to your child this week about the Bible being the word of God. Place the open Bible in your midst at family prayer time. Read a short passage from it each day.

Sincerely in Christ,
Teacher _____

Questions

Is the Bible divided into two parts?
Is the first part called the Old Testament?
Does the Old Testament tell us about the Savior coming into the world?
Is Jesus our Savior?
Is the Bible God's word?

THE SPIRIT OF THE LORD
Jim Strathdee

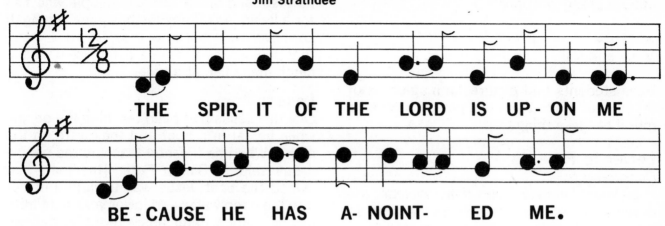

THE SPIR-IT OF THE LORD IS UP-ON ME

BE-CAUSE HE HAS A-NOINT-ED ME.

Cycle C
Fourth Sunday of Year

We Walk Away From the Anger of Others

Supplies Needed
magazines
glue
scissors
strip of brown wrapping paper

Liturgy
Gather around the altar. Join hands.

All:
I will sing of your salvation.

Sing:
"The Spirit of the Lord" and "Jesus Loves Me." (Use gestures.)
Jesus loves me, this I know (hug self)
for the Bible tells me so (hands held as though holding a book)
little ones to him belong (arms outstretched)
we are weak (go limp all over)
but he is strong. (hold arms up to show off muscle)

yes, Jesus loves me (repeat three times, hugging self, and nodding "yes")
for the Bible tells me so. (hands held as though holding a book)

Review
Using poster from last lesson to stimulate recall, ask the students to tell as much as they can remember of the lesson. Fill in the parts not remembered or repeat the story part.

Lesson
Jesus was teaching in the synagogue [church] in the town where he was raised. The people remembered him as the son of Joseph, the carpenter. They did not like to hear the things Jesus said to them. They became angry and took him up to the top of a hill intending to throw him over its edge, but Jesus walked through them and went away.

[That is what Jesus wants us to do. When someone becomes angry with us and wants to hurt us, we walk away rather than fight with them.]

Lesson (continued)
Let us go to our altar again. We will sit quietly for a few minutes and think of anyone we have ever hurt. [After a pause for reflection, say:] Let us say together, "Jesus, help me to

always be kind to everyone." [Give each other a greeting of peace.]

Activity
Make a mural.

Have students find pictures in magazines of things that make them feel peaceful. Make a mural of these things.

Letter to Parents
Dear Parents,

In your family prayer time, include the prayer "Jesus, help me always be kind to everyone" and a greeting of peace.

Sincerely in Christ,
Teacher _____

Questions
Did Jesus walk away when the people became angry with him?
Should we walk away when someone wants to fight us?
Should we be kind to everyone?

Cycle C
Fifth Sunday of Year

Jesus' Friends Tell Others About Jesus

Supplies Needed
roll of wax paper
small pieces of fern or ivy
fish cutouts (approximately 3 per student; see patterns, page 103)
iron
grocery sack to use as iron pad
1 can water-packed tuna
crackers (plain)
can opener
matching cards (from 3rd Sunday of Year—Cycle B)

Activity
Give each student a taste of tuna on a cracker. (Use water-packed tuna if any of your students is on a strict diet.) Talk about its taste and smell. Discuss people who fish for a living. Ask if anyone has gone fishing. If so, have them tell how they fished. Explain that people who fish for a living use nets and catch many fish at a time.

Lesson
One day Jesus had been teaching the people while he sat in a boat and they were on the shore. When he finished teaching the people Jesus said to Simon Peter [the man who owned the boat Jesus was using], "Put out into the deep water and lower your nets for a catch." Simon Peter answered, "Master, we have fished all night long and have caught nothing: but if you say so, I will lower the nets." Upon doing this they caught such a great number of fish that their nets were breaking. They signaled their friends in another boat to come and help them. The two boats were filled until they nearly sank. At the sight of this Simon Peter fell at the knees of Jesus saying, "Leave me, Lord. I am a sinful man." Jesus said, "Do not be afraid. From now on you will be catching men." [That was a strange thing Jesus said. He was telling the fishermen that he wanted them to come with him and tell others about Jesus.]

Activity
Matching cards (see 3rd Sunday of Year—Cycle B). Have a selection of fish shapes cut from various colors of construction paper (or let students cut out own). Let each student select approximately three fish. Place fish on top half of waxed paper (approximately 11" × 22"). Add bits of green fern or ivy. Fold bottom half up to cover arrangement. Place on folded grocery sack. With warm iron, press over entire piece of folded wax paper to seal. Have students take home to put in a window.

Liturgy
Gather around altar. Join hands.

All:
In the sight of angels I will sing your praises, Lord. Jesus, I love you. I want everyone to love you. I will tell my friends about you.

FISH PATTERNS FOR ACTIVITY

Cut of various colors of construction paper.

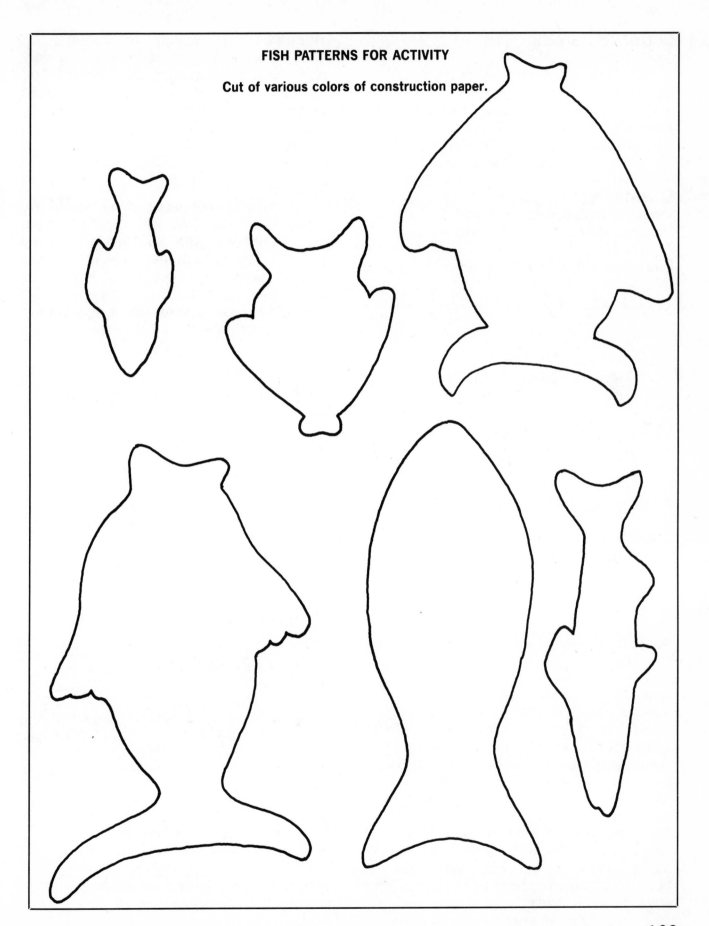

Letter to Parents

Dear Parents,

Today we heard the story of Jesus selecting his first Apostles. They would tell others about Jesus. This week in your family prayer time, sing: "Jesus is Lord."

Sincerely in Christ,
Teacher _____

Questions

Were the Apostles Jesus' friends?
Did they tell others about Jesus?
Are we Jesus' friends?
Should we tell others about Jesus?

Cycle C
Sixth Sunday of Year

We Share the Love of Jesus With Others

Supplies Needed

colored paper
lined paper
pictures from old greeting cards
pens
glue
scissors
crayolas

Lesson

Jesus came down the mountain to a place where his disciples [followers] were with many people. Jesus said: Blest are you poor, the reign of God is yours. [Jesus was saying: Blest are you poor for you have me.] Then Jesus said: Blest are you who hunger, filled you shall be. [Jesus fills us at communion.] Blest are you who are weeping, you shall laugh. [Jesus comforts us when we are unhappy.] Blest are you when men hate you because of me. Rejoice and be glad, for your reward shall be great in heaven.

Discuss

Jesus was telling us that he loves us very much. He understands all our problems. And if people tease us or make fun of us because we love Jesus, our reward in heaven will be great. Sing: "Joy, Joy, Joy" from *Hi God* record.

Activity

We have the love of Jesus in our hearts. We should share that love with others. We are going to share it with our friends from the nursing home. Each student makes a card or draws a picture or writes a note to the person he/she adopted at their visit earlier this year to the nursing home. (Be sure to take or mail the greetings to the shut-ins.)

Liturgy

Gather around altar. Sing: "Joy, Joy, Joy" again.

All:
Happy are they who hope in the Lord.

(Encourage the students to make up prayers telling Jesus how much they love him and to thank Jesus for loving them)

All:
Happy are they who hope in the Lord.

Letter to Parents

Dear Parents,

We are trying to build in the students a loving concern for others. If you know any shut-ins, visit them with your child this week.

Sincerely in Christ,
Teacher _____

Questions

Does Jesus love us very much?
Does Jesus understand us?
Does Jesus love and understand everyone?
Should we tell people that Jesus loves and understands them?

Cycle C
Seventh Sunday of Year

Love Everyone
Be Good to Everyone

Supplies Needed
12″ × 18″ sheet construction
paper (1 per student)
pictures of Jesus as an adult (1 per student)
magazines
glue or paste
felt pens
scissors
paste brushes or swabs

Lesson
One day Jesus said, "Do to others what you would have them do to you. It is easy to love someone who loves you. It is easy to be good to someone who is good to you. Love everyone. Be good to everyone as God your Father loves everyone and is good to everyone."

Liturgy
Gather around altar. Join hands.

Encourage the students to make up a prayer telling God how much they love him. Then teacher adds and students repeat: Dear Father, help me to love everyone. Help me to be good to everyone.

All
The Lord is kind and merciful.

Activity
Give each student a sheet of 12″ × 18″ construction paper. Have printed across 18″ side: JESUS LOVES EVERYONE. (Let students who are capable do own printing.) Each student pastes on a picture of Jesus as an adult. From magazines, students find pictures of people, all ages, and add these to their paper. Selection and arrangement of pictures should be students' own work.

Letter to Parents
Dear Parents,
The golden rule was our theme for today. In your family prayer time this week, include a request that God help us to love everyone and be good to everyone.
Sincerely in Christ,
Teacher _____

Questions
Does God the Father love everyone?
Is God the Father good to everyone?
Should we love everyone?
Should we be good to everyone?

Cycle C
Eighth Sunday of Year

We Try to
Correct Our Faults

Supplies Needed
one sheet poster board
magazines
scissors
glue
9″ × 12″ construction paper
note paper
pencils or pens
crayolas

Lesson
One day Jesus told his disciples [followers] "Why look at the speck in your brother's eye when you miss the plank [big board] in your own? How can you say to your brother, let me remove the speck from your eye? Yet fail to see the plank lodged in your own? Remove the plank from your own eye first." Jesus was telling us we should correct our own

faults [bad habits] before we tell others about their faults [bad habits].

Liturgy
Gather around altar. Sit quietly with eyes closed.

Teacher:
Let us quietly think about our own faults. (Pause.) Now let us say, "Jesus, I am sorry. Please forgive me. [Pause.] When we tell Jesus we are sorry and ask him to forgive us we know he does forgive us. Then we should thank Jesus."

All:
Lord, it is good to give thanks to you.

Sing:
Kumbaya: "Someone's thankful, Lord be with us."

Activity
Explain: One way to overcome our faults is to be helpful and thoughtful of others. Make one large collage of people who help others. Let students select pictures from magazines. Write notes or make greeting cards for our shut-in friends in the nursing home.

Letter to Parents
Dear Parents,

Today's lesson was about correcting our faults. Include a simple act of contrition in your family prayer.

Sincerely in Christ,
Teacher _____

Questions
Does Jesus want us to correct our own faults or bad habits?
Should we say, "Jesus, I am sorry"?
Does Jesus forgive us?
Should we thank Jesus for forgiving us?

Cycle C
Ninth Sunday of Year

Tell the Good News

Supplies Needed
poster board (1 per student)
scissors
marking pens
glue
pictures depicting the life of Christ (suggested greeting cards to collect for project: Easter; sympathy; and a few Christmas)
old religious calendar pictures (use only pictures depicting stories students have heard)

Lesson
We have often heard how much Jesus wants us to love everyone. Today's story is about a man who loved his servant [a man who worked for him]. A Centurion [Roman soldier] had a servant. The servant was sick and almost dead. When he heard about Jesus he sent some Jewish elders [leaders] to Jesus asking him to come and save the life of his servant. The Jewish elders told Jesus: "He deserves this favor from you because he loves our people and even built our synagogue [church] for us." [The Roman soldier had been kind to the people. He had built their church for them. The people loved the Roman soldier and went to Jesus for him.] Jesus set out with them. When he was a short distance from the house the Centurion sent friends to tell Jesus, "Sir, do not trouble yourself, for I am not worthy to have you enter my house. Just give the order and my servant will be cured." Jesus was amazed when he heard this and told the crowd following him, "I tell you I have never found so much faith among my own people." When the Centurion's friends returned to the house, they found the servant in perfect health.

The Roman soldier was from another country but his faith [belief] that Jesus was able to cure the servant was greater [stronger] than the faith of the people Jesus had been teaching.

Liturgy
Gather around altar.

All:
Go out to all the world and tell the Good News.

Teacher:
Part of the Good News is: Jesus cures the sick. (Ask students if they have any sick relatives or friends. Encourage each child to say a spontaneous prayer to Jesus for the health of the person named. If they do not seem able to do so, assist them with: Jesus, please make   [name]   well.")

Activity
Make a Good News poster.

Let each student make one. Have a selection of pictures for the students to choose from. Pictures should depict scenes from the life of Christ. Can be from greeting cards, holy cards and old religious calendars. Use only ones students understand. Be sure each student has one picture of Jesus crucified and Jesus risen. Other suggestions: Last Supper; birth of Christ. Have students print GOOD NEWS somewhere on their poster.

Letter to Parents
Dear Parents,
   Today we heard the story of the cure of the Centurion's servant. In your prayers this week, include prayers for sick relatives and friends.

Sincerely in Christ,
Teacher _____

Questions
Ask the students to tell what is taking place on each picture on their posters. After they explain each picture, state, "That is Good News."

Of all the Good News about Jesus, what is the best news? (Jesus died to save everyone.)

Cycle C
Tenth Sunday of Year

Jesus Is Lord

Supplies Needed
Hemmed material at least 8″ × 11″ (top hem 1″ deep)
Suggest: burlap or drapery samples, one per student.
Felt letters, one set per student (pattern, page 108)
¼″ dowel 9″ or 10″ long, one per student
Yarn or string for hanging, 2″ longer than dowel (one per student)
Glue

Lesson
Jesus went to a town called Naim, and his disciples and a large crowd went with him. As he neared the town a dead man was being carried out. He was the only son of a widowed mother [a woman whose husband is dead]. The Lord felt sorry when he saw her, and said, "Do not cry." Then he stepped forward and touched the litter [like a stretcher, on which they carried the dead man]. Jesus said, "Young man, I bid you get up." The dead man sat up and began to speak, then Jesus gave him back to his mother.

Discuss
Jesus made a dead man live again. Imagine how surprised the people were. Jesus was showing the people that he was special. Jesus is God, but the people did not realize that.

Liturgy
Gather around the altar. Join hands. Raise joined hands above heads.

All:
I will praise you, Lord, for you have rescued me.

Teacher:
Jesus, you are God.

All:
Jesus, you are God.

Teacher:
Jesus, you are Lord.

All:
Jesus, you are Lord.

All:
I will praise you, Lord, for you have rescued me.

Activity
Banner: JESUS IS LORD

Have students place letters in position so you can check for accuracy before gluing.

Letter to Parents
Dear Parents,

Jesus performed many miracles showing the people he was Lord, yet most did not realize who Jesus was. We must recognize Jesus is Lord. In your family prayer this week, include this simple prayer: "Jesus, you are Lord."

Sincerely in Christ,
Teacher _____

Questions
Is Jesus God?
Is Jesus Lord?

PATTERN FOR BANNER
Number under each letter indicates number needed for each student.

JESU I
1   2   3   1   1

LORD
1   1   1   1

Cycle C
Eleventh Sunday of Year

We Ask for Forgiveness

Supplies Needed
pieces of plywood or scrap lumber 5″ × 7″ (Lumber yards are good about donating scrap lumber and cutting it to size if you tell them what you want it for.)
sandpaper
toothpicks
picture hangers

hammer
small legumes (¼ cup makes 3 or 4 plaques); use beans, peas, lentils or the least expensive legume you can purchase. Rice is too small.
one set construction paper letters per student (see pattern, page 110)
one spray can clear acrylic enamel

Lesson
A certain Pharisee [leader of the people] invited Jesus to dinner. As they were at the table a sinful woman brought a vase of perfumed oil and stood behind Jesus at his feet, weeping so her tears fell upon his feet. Then she wiped them with her hair, kissing them and perfuming them with the oil. The Pharisee thought, "If he knew what kind of a woman she is he wouldn't let her touch him."

"Simon," Jesus said, "Two men owed money to a moneylender, one owed five hundred coins, the other fifty. Neither man was able to pay so the moneylender canceled each debt. Which man was the most grateful [thankful]?" Simon said, "The one who owed the most."

"That's right," Jesus said, "You see this woman? I came to your home and you gave

me no water to wash my feet." [In those days, people wore sandals and walked on dusty roads, so when guests came to visit, people offered them water to wash their feet.) "She has washed my feet with her tears and wiped them with her hair. You gave me no kiss but she has not stopped kissing my feet. You did not anoint my head with oil, but she has anointed my feet with perfume. I tell you, that is why her many sins are forgiven—because of her great love. Little is forgiven the one whose love is small." Jesus said to her, "Your sins are forgiven. Go now in peace."

Liturgy
Gather around altar. Sit on chairs, feet on floor, hands in lap in open prayer position, eyes closed. Ask students to think about any wrong they have done. Pause.

All:
Lord, forgive the wrong I have done. (Pause.)

Teacher:
Go in peace.

All:
Amen.

Activity
Make a PEACE plaque.

Sandpaper edges of wood until smooth and no danger of slivers. Place construction paper letters in place. Check for accuracy before gluing. Fasten hanger to back of plaque (important to do before gluing legumes). Glue legumes to letters on plaque. Use toothpick to help position legumes. When work is complete, take out of doors to spray with clear acrylic enamel.

Letter to Parents
Dear Parents,

Jesus preached forgiveness, but we must ask for it. Include in your family prayer the psalm: "Lord, Forgive the Wrong I Have Done."

Sincerely in Christ,
Teacher _____

Questions

Should we be sorry for any sins (wrongs) we commit?
Should we ask Jesus to forgive us?
Does Jesus give us peace?

PATTERN FOR PEACE PLAQUE

5″

7″

CYCLE A
First Sunday of Lent

We Pray When We Are Tempted

Fig. 1

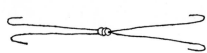

1. Twist two pipe cleaners together in center. (Fig. 1)

2. Bend each end up about 1″ to form hook. (Fig. 1)

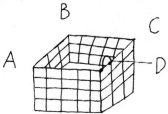

Fig. 2

Supplies Needed
old calendars (1 per student)
pencils
plastic strawberry baskets (1 per student)
ribbon, any color, pieces 18″ or longer
glue to fasten ribbon ends
2 *long* pipe cleaners per student

Activity
Have students mark off forty days on an old calendar.

Lesson
Jesus went into the desert for forty days to pray. During that time he ate nothing. [Check the days crossed off calendar.] Then the devil came and tempted Jesus [tried to get him to do wrong]. Three times he tempted Jesus but Jesus sent the devil away.

Liturgy
Gather around altar.

Teacher:
Many times we are tempted to do something wrong. We should pray then.

All:
Be with me, Lord, when I am in trouble. [Close eyes; sit quietly and invite Jesus into your heart.]

All:
Thank you, Jesus, for being with me always.

Activity
Begin Easter baskets for our shut-in friends. Use plastic strawberry baskets. Use long colored pipe cleaners to make handle.

3. Fasten to basket at each corner. (Points A,B,C,D) (Fig. 2)

4. Twist to secure. Optional: Add a bow to center of handle.

5. Weave ribbon through mesh of basket. Weaving is easier if one hand is inside basket and one hand outside.

6. Glue ribbon ends to secure. Paper ribbon is good to use but not the narrow ribbon that curls.

7. Label baskets for completion at next class.

Letter to Parents
Dear Parents,
   This week we learned we should pray when tempted. In your family prayer time this week, include the psalm: "Be with Me, Lord, When I Am in Trouble."
                    Sincerely in Christ,
                    Teacher _____

Questions
Should we pray when we are tempted?
Will Jesus help us?
Is Jesus with us always?

CYCLE C
Second Sunday of Lent

We Can Pray Anywhere

Supplies Needed
hosiery eggs (1 per student)
Tissue paper cut into circles, squares, triangles, flowers, or other shapes, approximately 2" in diameter. Use many colors.
glue

Lesson
Jesus took three of his disciples, Peter, John, and James, and went up onto a mountain to pray. While he was praying his face changed in appearance and his clothes became dazzlingly white [so bright it was hard to look at them]. Then from a cloud came a voice which said, "This is my son, my chosen one. Listen to him." When the voice became silent, Jesus was there as he had always been.

Discuss
Why did Jesus go up the mountain? (To pray.) Have you ever been in the mountains? (If not, ask: Have you ever been in the woods or a lovely park? Compare to being in the mountains.) While you were there, did you pray? The outdoors is a wonderful place to pray.

Liturgy
Go to the school yard or a nearby park or a neighboring yard. See the beautiful plants and smell them. Say a prayer. Encourage the students to make up a prayer. Listen with eyes closed to the sounds of nature (birds; breeze; rustle of the leaves; crickets; frogs; etc.).

Make up more prayers after listening. Close with all saying: The Lord is my light and my salvation.

Activity
Continue Easter baskets.

To make egg for basket: Using hosiery eggs, cover a small area with a thin layer of glue. Press pre-cut shapes of tissue paper over glue area. Repeat until both sections of egg are decorated. Tissue paper bleeds easy. Be sure glue on egg is not too thick or the results will be messy. Additional decorations can be glued on egg if student wishes. Let work be students' own creative ideas. (Project will be completed at next class.)

Letter to Parents
Dear Parents,
Have your family prayer time outside if possible and given thanks for all of nature.
Sincerely in Christ,
Teacher _____
N.B. Next week we will need parents to transport students to visit the nursing home.

Questions
Can we pray anywhere we are?
Name some places we can pray.

Cycle C
Third Sunday of Lent

The Lord Is Kind and Merciful

Supplies Needed
artificial grass
jelly beans
figs or fig cookies (1 per student)
parents to transport students to nursing home

Activity
Begin class by sharing some figs. (If figs are not available, give each student a fig cookie.) Break open. Smell fruit and taste it. Discuss the smell and taste.

Lesson
Jesus told a parable [riddle-like story]. A man had a fig tree growing in his yard, and he came out to look for fruit on it but did not

find any. He said to one of his workers, "Look here! for three years now I have come looking for fruit on this tree and found none. Cut it down." In answer his worker said, "Sir, leave it another year while I hoe around it and manure [fertilize] it; then perhaps it will bear fruit. If not, it shall be cut down."

Discuss
Once again Jesus was telling the people to change their ways of living, to become better people. He compared the people to the fig tree. It had no fruit. The people were not being good. Jesus was telling them to be better or he would have nothing to do with them.

Liturgy
Gather around altar. All join hands.

Teacher:
In today's story the man gave the fig tree another chance to bear fruit. Every day we have another chance to be a better person. (All close eyes and think about being a better person.)

All:
The Lord is kind and merciful.

Activity
Put artificial grass in baskets. Fill decorated eggs with jelly beans. (This can be a very good lesson in unselfishness and sharing if you have just enough jelly beans to fill the eggs.)

Take the baskets to our shut-in friends in the nursing home. (Make arrangements ahead of time for this visit.)

Letter to Parents
Dear Parents,
   We are still hearing Jesus' message to reform our lives. Include the psalm "The Lord Is Kind and Merciful" in your family prayer this week.

Sincerely in Christ,
Teacher _____

Questions
Is Jesus kind and merciful?
Does Jesus give us another chance?

Cycle C
Fourth Sunday of Lent

God Is Pleased with Us When We Say, "I Am Sorry"

Supplies Needed
cookies
party hats
paper napkins
juice
favors
paper cups

Activity
When students arrive, have room ready for a party. Put party hats on each student. Have table set with cookies, juice and favors at each place. Enjoy the party. When the students have enjoyed themselves, tell the story of the Prodigal Son.

Lesson
One day Jesus told this parable [riddle-like story]. A man had two sons. The younger son said to his father, "Give me my share of the property." So the father divided everything. The son took all his belongings and went off to another land. Here he wasted all his money. After he had spent all his money a great famine broke out. [A famine is a time when a country cannot grow enough food to feed the people.] The boy got a job on a farm feeding the pigs. But the boy was hungry and wished he could eat the pig's food. Then he thought of his father's home. There the workers had more to eat than the boy did. The boy decided to go back to his father and say, "Father, I have sinned against God and you. I no longer deserve to be called your son. Treat me like one of your workers." With that he set off for his father's house. His

father saw him coming and ran out to meet him, threw his arms around him and kissed him.

The son said, "Father, I have sinned against God and against you, I no longer deserve to be called your son." The father told his servants [workers], "Quick, bring out the finest robe and put it on him, put a ring on his finger and shoes on his feet. Let us eat and celebrate [have a party] because this son of mine was dead and has come back to life, was lost and is found." Then the celebration [party] began.

Discuss
Was it easy for the boy to tell his father he had done wrong? Talk about admitting our mistakes. Stress: God is pleased with us when we say we are sorry.

Liturgy
Gather around the altar.

All:
Taste and see the goodness of the Lord.

Teacher:
Dear God, give us the courage to say, "I am sorry."

All:
Taste and see the goodness of the Lord.

Letter to Parents
Dear Parents,
Repentance is the theme of Lent. Continue to include prayers of contrition and thanksgiving for God's mercy in your family prayer time.

Sincerely in Christ,
Teacher _____

Questions
Is it easy to say, "I was wrong"?
Is it easy to say, "I am sorry"?
Is God pleased with us when we say, "I am sorry"?

Cycle C
Fifth Sunday of Lent

Jesus Forgives Us When We Say, "I Am Sorry"

Supplies Needed
8" × 10" piece of plywood per student
sandpaper
plaque hanger
glue
hammer
one spray can clear acrylic enamel
dried legumes (¼ cup per two students)
one set construction paper letters per student (see pattern, page 115)

Discuss
Last week we heard the story of the young man who went away, then returned home to tell his father he was sorry. Today's story is also about being sorry.

Lesson
One day as Jesus was teaching the people some men brought to Jesus a woman who had been caught sinning. They said to Jesus, "This woman was caught sinning. The law says she must be stoned. What do you say?" Jesus knew they were trying to trap him. Jesus bent down and began to write in the sand. Then he said, "Let the man among you who has not sinned throw the first stone." One by one the men slipped away. Soon only the woman was left with Jesus. He asked her, "Where did they all go? Has no one condemned you?" "No one, sir," she answered. "Nor do I condemn you. You may go, but from now on avoid this sin."

Discuss
Is it hard to say, "I am sorry" to someone else? Is it easier to point and say, "He did it" or "She did it"? That is what the men in the story today did. They didn't want to admit

they had done wrong. It was easier to point to the woman and say, "She did it." What did Jesus do? Did Jesus forgive the woman?

Liturgy
Gather around altar. Sit with eyes closed.

Teacher:
Jesus forgives us when we tell him we are sorry. Let us think quietly about any wrongs we have done. [Pause for a couple minutes.] Now let us tell Jesus, quietly in our hearts, that we are sorry. [Pause.]

All:
The Lord has done great things for us; we are filled with joy.

Sing:
Kumbaya: "Someone's joyful, Lord, be with us."

Activity
Joy plaques.

Sandpaper edges of boards until smooth.

Attach hanger to back.

Place construction paper letters on board. Check for accuracy.

Glue construction paper letters to board.

Over letters glue beans, corn or split peas.

When complete, take outside and spray with clear acrylic enamel.

Letter to Parents
Dear Parents,
The plaque your child made this week expresses our feelings at God's forgiveness.

**Pattern for
Joy plaque
Cut one set of letters per student.
Make of construction paper.**

Include in your family prayer this week: "The Lord has done great things for us, we are filled with joy."

Sincerely in Christ,
Teacher _____

Questions
Is it easy to point to someone and say, "He or she did it"?

Is it hard to say, "I am sorry" to someone else?

Does Jesus forgive us when we say, "I am sorry"?

PALM SUNDAY—Same as Cycle A and B
For lesson, see Palm Sunday—Cycle A.

No class for Easter Sunday.

SECOND SUNDAY OF EASTER—Same all three cycles A, B, and C.
For lesson, see Second Sunday of Easter—Cycle A.

Cycle C
Third Sunday of Easter

We Will Try to Be Like Jesus

Supplies Needed
soft French rolls
water-packed tuna
Enough so each student may have a small snack.

Discuss
Fishing. Ask if anyone has ever gone fishing. Let the students tell of their experiences. Have them describe the method of fishing. Explain the use of nets used by commercial fishermen. Several of the Apostles were commercial fishermen.

Lesson
One day Peter and some of the other disciples decided to go fishing. They fished all night but caught nothing. At daybreak Jesus was standing on the shore but they did not know it was Jesus. Jesus said, "Children, have you caught anything to eat?" "Not a thing," they answered. "Cast your net on the starboard side [right side] and you will find something," Jesus told them. They made a cast [threw out their net] and caught so many fish they could not haul the net in. One disciple called out, "It is the Lord." On hearing this Peter jumped into the water to go to Jesus. The other disciples brought in the boat dragging the net full of fish. When they landed, Jesus had a fire burning with some fish and bread on it. "Bring some of the fish you just caught," Jesus said. Then Jesus gave them some of the bread to eat and some of the fish. This was the third time Jesus appeared to his disciples after being raised from the dead.

Discuss
The disciples had fished all night. Do you think they were hungry and tired? Have you ever been hungry and tired? Did someone have you sit down and serve you food? How did it feel? The person who served you was being kind and thoughtful. Jesus had prepared fish and bread for his disciples. Jesus was kind and thoughtful.

Activity
Serve students bread and fish. Use canned tuna (water-packed) and soft French rolls broken in small pieces.

Discuss While Eating
The disciples were happy to see Jesus because he served them food while they rested, but they were more happy because Jesus, their friend whom they loved, was with them. Jesus who had died, had risen from the dead. Jesus had returned to them alive.

Liturgy
Gather around altar. Join hands.

All:
I will praise you,
Lord, for you have rescued me.

116

Jesus, thank you for dying for us.
Jesus, thank you for rising again.
Jesus, I want to be like you.
Jesus, I will be kind and thoughtful.

Sing:
Let heaven rejoice and earth be glad,
Let all creation sing.
Let children proclaim through ev'ry land,
"Hosanna to our King."

Letter to Parents
Dear Parents,
Today we saw an example of Jesus' kindness and thoughtfulness. This week, encourage your child to perform acts of kindness and thoughtfulness, for we are trying to be like Jesus.

Sincerely in Christ,
Teacher _____

Questions
Was Jesus kind to others?
Was Jesus thoughtful of others?
Should we be kind to others?
Should we be thoughtful of others?

Cycle C
Fourth Sunday of Easter

We Belong to Jesus, as the Sheep Belong to the Shepherd

Supplies Needed
8" × 10" board (1 per student)
sandpaper
hammer
round toothpicks
picture hangers
clear drying glue
1 can clear acrylic enamel
white construction paper sheep cutout (1 per student), see pattern, page 75

macaroni (medium-sized elbow) ⅓ cup per student
lentils (approximately 45 per student)

Begin Class
By encouraging students to tell about any acts of kindness or thoughtfulness they did the past week.

Lesson
Jesus said: "My sheep hear my voice, I know them, and they follow me. I give them eternal life and they shall never perish [die forever]. No one shall snatch them out of my hand. My Father is greater than all, in what he has given me, and there is no snatching out of his hand. The Father and I are one.

Discuss
Jesus calls us his sheep. If we follow him we will one day live with him forever in heaven. We belong to Jesus and his Father. Who is Jesus' Father? (God.) No one can take us away from Jesus or his Father.

Liturgy
Gather around altar.

All:
We are his people, the sheep of his flock.

Leader:
Jesus, we belong to you.

All:
We are his people, the sheep of his flock.

Leader:
Jesus, we will follow you.

All:
We are his people, the sheep of his flock.

Leader:
Jesus, no one can take us away from you.

All:
We are his people, the sheep of his flock.

Activity
Sheep plaque.

Sandpaper edges of board until smooth.

Students glue construction paper sheep cutouts to board.

Attach hanger to back. (It is important that this step be done before macaroni is glued to picture.)

Use clear drying glue. Glue lentils to hooves, eye, and inner ear. Use toothpicks to help position.

Glue elbow macaroni onto sheep cutout.

When complete, spray with clear acrylic enamel. (Do this step outdoors.)

Letter to Parents
Dear Parents,

This week in your family prayer include the psalm: "We Are His People, the Sheep of His Flock."

Sincerely in Christ,
Teacher _____

N.B. Next week we need parents to assist in transporting students to visit the nursing home.

Questions
Do we belong to Jesus and his Father?
Who Is Jesus' Father?
Can anyone take us away from Jesus?

Cycle C
Fifth Sunday of Easter

Jesus Wants Us to Love Everyone

Supplies Needed
sewing cards (see pattern and instructions, page 119),
1 per student
yarn 4½ feet long (1 per student)
blunt tapestry needle (1 per student)
parents willing to transport students to nursing home

Lesson
At the Last Supper, Jesus told his disciples, "My children, I am not to be with you much longer. I give you a new commandment. Love one another. Such as my love has been for you so must your love be for each other. That is how all will know you are my disciples by your love for one another."

Stress
We love our families. We love our friends. Jesus wants us to love everyone.

Liturgy
Gather around altar.

All:
I will praise your name forever, my King and my God.

Sing:
"Thank you, God, For Giving Us Us" from "Hi God."

Activity
Work sewing cards.
Take to nursing home friend.

Letter to Parents
Dear Parents,

We must love everyone. Continue to encourage your child to be kind and thoughtful to others.

Sincerely in Christ,
Teacher _____

Questions
Do we love our parents?
Do we love our brothers? Sisters?
Do we love our friends?
Should we love everyone?

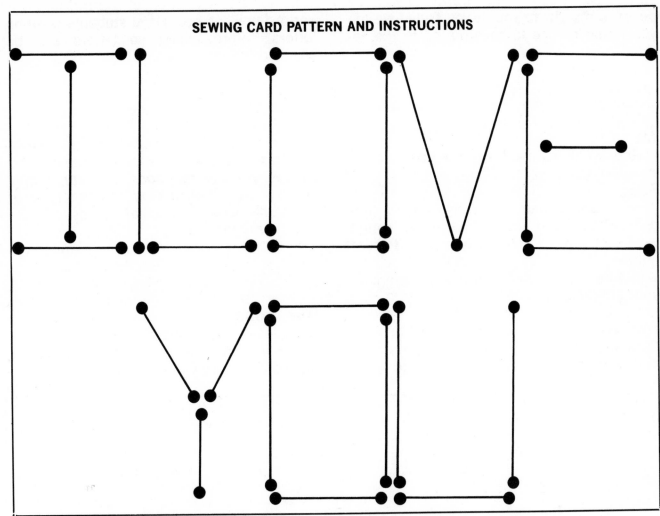

SEWING CARD PATTERN AND INSTRUCTIONS

1. Use cards from hosiery packages. 2. With a sharp tapestry needle, punch holes.
3. Draw lines for students to follow. Do steps 1, 2, and 3 prior to class.
4. Student uses blunt tapestry needle and 4½ ft. of yarn to sew card.

Cycle C
Sixth Sunday of Easter

With the Peace of Jesus in our Hearts We Praise God

Supplies Needed
pre-cut red felt heart (1 per student)
alphabet macaroni (Have letters needed, pre-sorted. Place in individual nut cups for safe keeping and easy use by students.) Letters needed: Praise God.
thin flat magnet strip (can be purchased at hobby or craft shop and cut with scissors)
glue

Lesson
Jesus would soon be leaving his disciples to return to his Father in heaven. He was trying to prepare them for when he would leave, so one day Jesus said to his disciples: "Anyone who loves me will be true to my word and my Father will love him: we will come to him and live with him always. [Everyone who loves Jesus clap your hands.] Then Jesus said: "The Holy Spirit, whom the Father will send in my name, will teach you in everything. [Jesus sent the Holy Spirit to live in us. The Holy Spirit helps us to learn about God.]

Jesus said: "Peace is my farewell to you, my peace is my gift to you. If you truly love me you would rejoice to have me go to the Father."

Liturgy
Gather around altar.

All:
O God, let all the nations praise you.

Sing:
"Praise God"; tune: "Amazing Grace." (Repeat "Praise God" throughout entire song.) Give each other a greeting of peace. Be sure students say, "May the peace of Jesus be with you." Be careful to include everyone in your greetings.

Activity
Glue macaroni letters on pre-cut red felt hearts. Praise God. Glue flat magnet to back.

Take home to attach to refrigerator door for entire family to see. Have students position letters before gluing so letters can be checked for accuracy.

Letter to Parents
Dear Parents,

Your child is bringing home a special project to share with the family. Please put it on the refrigerator door. In your family prayer, sing "Praise God" to the tune of "Amazing Grace." Repeat words "Praise God" throughout song.

Sincerely in Christ,
Teacher _____

Questions
Does Jesus give us his peace?
Do we have the peace of Jesus in our hearts?
Should we praise God?

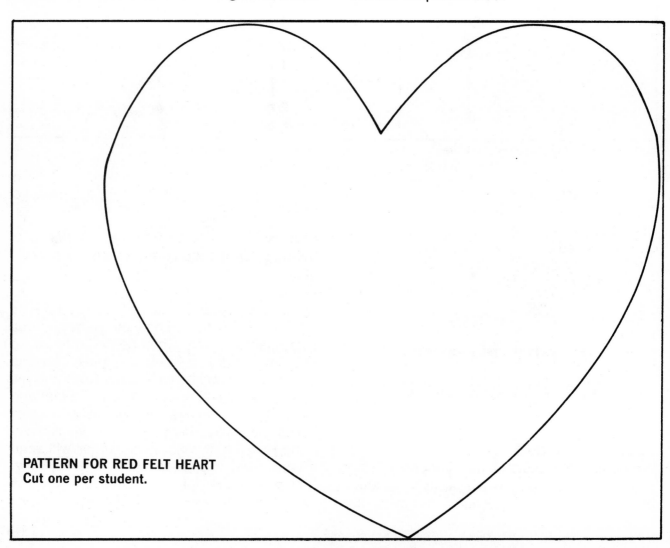

PATTERN FOR RED FELT HEART
Cut one per student.

Cycle C
Seventh Sunday of Easter

Jesus and God the Father Love Us. We Belong to Jesus and God the Father.

Supplies Needed
3" × 5" cards saying God loves you
string
balloons
small tank of helium
paper cups
punch
cookies
napkins
a parent willing to operate helium tank

Begin class
By gathering around the altar.

Teacher:
Today we will join Jesus in a prayer he said.

Lesson and Liturgy

Leader:
Jesus looked up to heaven and said: I do not pray for my disciples alone. I pray for those who will believe in me.

Teacher:
Jesus was praying for everyone who would ever believe in him. Jesus was praying for us.

All:
The Lord is king, the most high over all the earth.

Leader:
That all may be one as you, Father, are in me and I in you; I pray that they may be one in us.

Teacher:
Jesus and God the Father belong to each other. We belong to Jesus and God the father.

All:
The Lord is king, the most high over all the earth.

Leader:
That they may be one, as we are one—I living in them, you living in me.

Teacher:
Jesus lives in our hearts. We are in Jesus' heart.

All:
The Lord is king, the most high over all the earth.

Leader:
So shall the world know that you sent me, and that you loved them as you loved me.

Teacher:
God the Father loves us as he loves Jesus.

All:
The Lord is king, the most high over all the earth.

Activity
Celebrate God's love. Fill balloons with helium. Attach cards that say God loves you. Take out doors and release them. Have punch and cookies.

Letter to Parents
Dear Parents,
We belong to Jesus and God the Father. Include prayers of praise and thanksgiving for such a wonderful gift in your family prayer time this week.
Sincerely in Christ,
Teacher _____

Questions
Did Jesus pray for us?
Do we belong to Jesus and God the Father?
Are we in Jesus' heart?
Is Jesus in our hearts?
Does God the Father love us?

PENTECOST SUNDAY same as Cycle A—see page 31.

TRINITY SUNDAY same as Cycle A—see page 32.

Cycle C
Twenty-third Sunday of Year

We Pray for Strength and Courage to Follow Jesus

Supplies Needed
none

Activity
Play a game of follow the leader. Play outside; use playground equipment, i.e., swings, slide, etc. Have leader include somersaults, etc., so following is not easy but also not dangerous.

Lesson
Jesus told a large crowd of people, "If anyone comes to me without turning his back on his father and mother, his wife and his children, his brothers and sisters, indeed his very self, he cannot be my follower." [That was a strange thing for Jesus to say. He was telling the people that to follow him we must love Jesus enough to be willing to give up everything else we love just for Jesus.]

Then Jesus said, "If anyone does not take up his cross and follow me he cannot be my disciple." [Jesus was saying it is not always easy to follow him. Sometimes it is much easier to do something we should not do.]

Liturgy
Gather around altar.

All:
Jesus, I want to follow you.
Sometimes it is not easy.
Jesus, give me strength and courage to follow you.
In every age, O Lord, you have been our refuge.

Letter to Parents
Dear Parents,
It is not easy to take up our cross and follow Jesus. In your family prayer time this week, include prayers of petition for the strength and courage to follow Jesus.
Sincerely in Christ,
Teacher _____

Questions
Is it easy to follow Jesus?
Will Jesus help us if we ask?

Cycle C
Twenty-fourth Sunday of Year

No Matter How Bad We Are Jesus Loves Us and Wants Us to Repent

Supplies Needed
Shrink art plastic (packages of ten sheets can be purchased at hobby or craft stores). Cut each sheet into quarters.
Need ¼ sheet per student.
lamb pattern for each student
permanent felt-tip marker, fine point
paper punch
foil pie tins, several
oven thermometer
Make arrangements ahead of time to hold your class in the parish hall kitchen or someone's home or bring an electric toaster oven to class. Check oven you plan to use ahead of time to be sure it maintains a 300°F heat.

Lesson

Tax collectors and sinners were all gathered around Jesus to hear him. The Pharisees and Scribes [leaders of the people] murmured, "This man welcomes sinners and eats with them."

Then Jesus told a parable [story with a hidden meaning]. "Who among you if you had 100 sheep and lost one would not leave the 99 and go look for the one that was lost? And when he finds it, puts it on his shoulders with joy. Once home you would invite friends and neighbors in and say to them, 'Rejoice with me for I have found my lost sheep.' I tell you there will be more joy in heaven over one repentant sinner [one who says, 'I am sorry'] than over ninety nine who have no need of repentance."

Liturgy

Gather around altar. Join hands.

Leader:
No matter how bad we are, Jesus, you love us.

All:
I will rise and go to my Father.

Leader:
Help me, Jesus, to be a better person.

All:
I will rise and go to my Father.

Leader:
Lead me, Jesus, to God our Father.

All:
I will rise and go to my Father.

Activity

Shrink art.

Lay pieces of plastic over lamb pattern.

With permanent felt-tip marker student traces lamb onto plastic.

With paper punch, punch a hole in top of plastic. (If hole is to close to edge, it will leave a V shape instead of hole, so punch deep.)

Place plastic on foil pie tin in oven for 3 minutes at 300°F. (Be sure oven is 300°. If too cold, plastic won't shrink; if too hot, plastic will curl.) When complete, it can be used as a Christmas tree ornament or worn around the neck on a cord.

LAMB PATTERN FOR SHRINK ART

Letter to Parents

Dear Parents,
  No matter how bad we are Jesus loves us and wants us to repent. Include an act of contrition in your family prayers this week.
           Sincerely in Christ,
           Teacher _____

Questions

Does Jesus love us even when we are bad?
Does Jesus want us to say, "I am sorry"?
Does Jesus want us to try to be better?

Cycle C
Twenty-fifth Sunday of Year

We Trust In God

Supplies Needed
blindfolds for half the class

Activity
Trust walk. Blindfold half the class. Other half partners blindfolded students. Take a walk. Change roles. Discuss: How it feels to trust another. How it feels to be trusted.

Lesson
One day Jesus told his friends [apostles and disciples] that if a person was faithful [true] in little things then that person would be faithful [true] in big things. If a person was unjust [unkind] in little things that person would be unjust [unkind] in big things. Jesus said we cannot love both God and money. God must come first. God should be able to trust us, for we know we can trust God.

Liturgy
Gather around altar. Join hands.

Leader:
Dear God, we love you.

All:
Praise the Lord who lifts up the poor.

Leader:
Dear God, we know we can trust you for your word is true.

All:
Praise the Lord who lifts up the poor.

Leader:
Dear God, we will be kind.

All:
Praise the Lord who lifts up the poor.

Leader:
Dear God, we will be true.

All:
Praise the Lord who lifts up the poor.

Leader:
Jesus, we love you.

All:
Praise the Lord who lifts up the poor.

Sing:
"He's Got the Whole World in His Hands" and "Put Your Hand in the Hand." (Use gestures.)

Words and Gestures
HE'S GOT THE WHOLE WORLD (arms above head move in opposite directions to make a circle)
IN HIS HANDS (as hands meet extend straight out, palms up)
(Repeat four times.)
HE'S GOT YOU (point to others)
AND ME, BROTHER (point to self)
IN HIS HANDS (hands extended together, palms up)
(Repeat three times, end with "whole world" as above.)
HE'S GOT THE LITTLE BITTY BABY IN HIS HANDS (cradle arms)
(Repeat three times. End with "whole world" as above.)

Put Your Hand in the Hand
(Begin by extending left hand.)
PUT YOUR HAND (place right hand into left hand)
IN THE HAND (change hand positions and repeat above gesture)
OF THE MAN (both hands outline body shape)
WHO STILLED THE WATERS (hands extended, palms down, move in straight line to each side.)
PUT YOUR HAND (place right hand into left hand)
IN THE HAND (change hand positions and repeat above gesture)
OF THE MAN (both hands outline body shape)
WHO CALMED THE SEA (hands extended, palms down, move in straight line to each side.)

TAKE A LOOK AT YOUR SELF AND YOU CAN LOOK AT OTHERS DIFFERENTLY (hand at forehead shading eyes look from side to side)
PUT YOUR HAND (place right hand into left hand)
IN THE HAND (change positions of hand and repeat above)
OF THE MAN (both hands outline body shape)
FROM GALILEE. (hands extended, palms down, move in straight line to each side)

Letter to Parents

Dear Parents,

Today we learned that we can trust God. God wants to trust us. This week, place trust in your child, letting him/her know you are trusting him/her whether it be a small or large trust.

Sincerely in Christ,
Teacher _____

Questions

Can we trust God?
Is Jesus God?
Can we trust Jesus?
Can God trust us?

Cycle C
Twenty-sixth Sunday of Year

We Must Share We Must Listen to Our Parents and Teachers

Supplies Needed

graham crackers (½ enough for class)
brown wrapping paper (one strip long enough so each student has work area)
magazines
scissors
crayolas
thumb tacks

Activity

Pair students up. Pass out graham crackers to share. Sing during sharing.

Song:

(Tune: "Mulberry Bush")
This is the way we share our food
Share our food, share our food.
This is the way we share our food
As Jesus asked us to.

Song:

Kumbaya
Someone's sharing, Lord, be with us, etc.

Lesson

Jesus told a story of a rich man who had beautiful clothes, a nice house and plenty of food but he was very selfish. A poor man begged every day for just the food that fell off the table but the rich man would not give him even that. Both men died. The poor man went to heaven but the rich man did not.

The rich man asked God to send someone to warn his brothers not to be selfish as he was. But God said, "No, they have prophets [teachers] to tell them. They must listen to the prophets [teachers]."

Discuss

Sharing at home (toys, treats, etc.). Talk about saving stamps for poor missions. Have students save them this week and bring to next class. God wants us to share. We must not be selfish.

Discuss

Sharing vs. selfish.
What does sharing mean?
What does selfish mean?

God wants us to listen to our parents and teachers when they tell us how to be good, as the prophets did.

Liturgy

Gather around altar.

All:

Thank you God for all the nice things we have.

(Pause here and have students name some of the things they are thankful for.)

All:
Dear God, I will not be selfish. Praise the Lord, my soul.

Activity
Make a mural of people sharing and helping. (Encourage students to share working space, magazines, glue and crayolas.)

Use a strip of brown wrapping paper long enough so each student has a work area. Cut pictures from magazines of people sharing and helping and/or draw pictures. Hang in classroom when complete.

Letter to Parents
Dear Parents,
Our lesson today was on sharing and un-selfishness. This week encourage your child to share, cheerfully and willingly, each time an opportunity arises.
Sincerely in Christ,
Teacher _____

Questions
Does God want us to share what we have?
Did God give us parents to teach us how to be good?
Did God give us teachers to teach us how to be good?
Does God want us to listen to our parents and teachers?

Cycle C
Twenty-seventh Sunday of Year

We Must Do More Than Our Duty

Supplies Needed
3" × 5" lined index cards (1 per student)
pencils

Review
Obeying.

Do you have special chores to do? Name them or tell us about them. Should we expect Mother or Dad to say "Thank you" every time we do only our chores (duty)?

No, but some times if we surprise Mother or Dad and do something extra they will be happy and say, "Thank you." Then we are happy also.

Lesson
Jesus asked, "Would a man be grateful to a servant [one who works for him] who only carried out his orders? It is the same with you who hear me. When you have done all you have been commanded [told] to do, say "We are useless, we have done no more than our duty" [that which we are supposed to do].

Activity
Go back to chores students have mentioned and decide what additional things they can do this next week. On index cards, print the added chore to do this week. THIS WEEK I WILL _____. Take home to parents.

Liturgy
Gather around altar. Join hands.

All:
Jesus, you tell us to love others.
Jesus, you tell us to help others.
I will try to do my chores cheerfully because I love you and my parents.
This week I will do something extra for my parents.
If today you hear his voice, harden not your hearts.

Letter to Parents
Dear Parents,
The task mentioned on the card your child is bringing home today is one your child chose. Encourage him/her to do this additional task and be sure to thank him/her when it is done.
Sincerely in Christ,
Teacher _____

Questions

Do we all have special chores to do?
Do we do them willingly and cheerfully?
Should we try to do more than just what we are supposed to do?

Cycle C
Twenty-eighth Sunday of Year

We Tell God of Our Needs and Thank Him

Supplies Needed

crayolas
magazines
1 sheet of poster board
scissors
glue

Lesson

As Jesus was walking along ten lepers met him. [Lepers were people with a sickness no medicine could cure and it was easy for other people to get such a sickness.] The lepers kept their distance, raised their voices and said, "Jesus, Master, have pity on us!" When Jesus saw them, he said, "Go and show yourselves to the priests." On their way they were cured [made well]. One of them realizing that he had been cured, came back praising God in a loud voice.

Jesus said, "Were not all ten made well? Where are the other nine?" Jesus said to the man, "Stand up and go your way; your faith has been your salvation [saved you]."

Liturgy

Gather around altar.

Teacher:

Jesus could see the men had a disease, but he did not cure them until they asked. God wants us to ask for our needs.

All:

(Encourage the students to make up prayers of petition, especially for the needs of others.)

Teacher:

Only one man came back to thank Jesus. God wants us all to thank him.

All:

(Make up prayers of thanksgiving.)

All:

The Lord has revealed to the nations his saving power.

Activity

Make a collage of things we are grateful for. (Class activity. Make one large collage.)

Letter to Parents

Dear Parents,
  God wants us to ask him for our needs and to thank him for our blessings. This week in your family prayer time, include prayers of petition, especially for others, and prayers of thanksgiving.

  Sincerely in Christ,
  Teacher _____

Questions

Does Jesus want to help us?
Does Jesus want us to ask when we need help?
Should we thank Jesus for the things he has done for us?

Cycle C
Twenty-ninth Sunday of Year

Keep Praying and God Will Answer

Supplies Needed

white construction paper
(1 sheet per student)
pencils
marking pens

Lesson

Jesus told a story about a mean old judge who did not want to help a poor widow lady [a woman whose husband is dead] get what was rightfully hers [really belonged to her]. Everyday the poor lady went back to see him and ask his help. Finally he got so tired of her pestering him he helped her. Jesus said to think how much quicker God who loves us will answer our prayers. Keep praying and God will answer us.

Liturgy

Gather around altar. Join hands.

(Have each student make up a prayer of petition and/or thanksgiving.) After each all respond with:

Our help is from the Lord who made heaven and earth.

Activity

Give each student a sheet of paper on which he/she prints: WHEN I PRAY GOD ANSWERS ME. Prepare some for students who cannot copy printing. Have students draw around the fingers of their own hands to make praying hands. (See pattern on this page)

Letter to Parents

Dear Parents,

Again our lesson was about praying. Continue in your prayers of petition and thanksgiving at your family prayer time this week.

Sincerely in Christ,
Teacher _____

Questions

Does God love us?
Will God answer us if we keep praying?

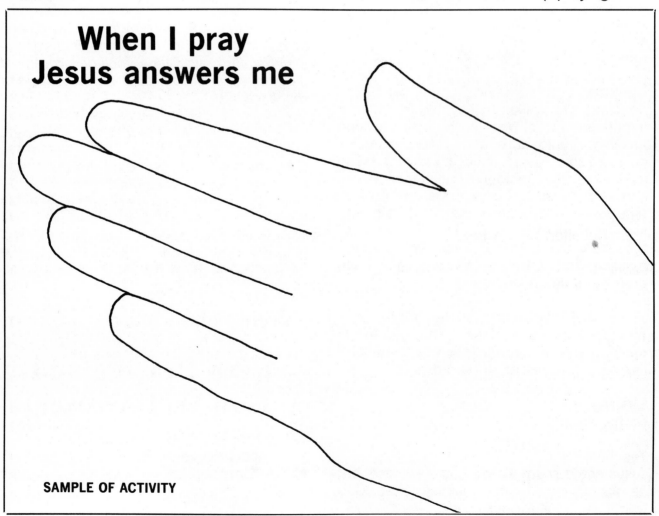

When I pray Jesus answers me

SAMPLE OF ACTIVITY

Cycle C
Thirtieth Sunday of Year

When I Say I Am Sorry God Forgives Me

Supplies Needed
matching cards (instructions on how to make and use on page 2.)
Words for matching cards: WHEN I SAY I AM SORRY GOD FORGIVES ME.

Lesson
Two men went to the temple [church] to pray. One man stood up in front so proud and said, "God, I thank you that I am so good. I'm better than other men. I am much better than that man in the back of the temple."

In the back of the temple the other man knelt to pray. He said, "God, I am sorry for every wrong I have ever done. Please forgive me."

Who do you think went home the happiest? Why? (Because he knew God loved him for saying, "I am sorry" and forgave him.)

Liturgy
Sit around altar. Close eyes.

Teacher:
Let us think about any wrong we have done. (Pause.)

All:
The Lord hears the cry of the poor. Lord, hear me as I say I am sorry.

Activity
Matching cards.
When I say I am sorry God forgives me.

Letter to Parents
Dear Parents,
When we say, "I am sorry," God forgives us. Include in your family prayer time a prayer of contrition and a prayer of thanksgiving for God's loving forgiveness.
Sincerely in Christ,
Teacher _____

Questions
When I do wrong, should I say, "I am sorry"?
Will God forgive me if I say, "I am sorry"?

Cycle C
Thirty-first Sunday of Year

God Loves Us and Forgives Us

Supplies Needed
matching cards from last lesson
record: "Joy Is like the Rain"

Lesson
There was a man named Zacchaeus, a tax collector and very rich. He was trying to see what Jesus was like but being rather small he was unable to do so because of the crowd. He climbed a tree near the road Jesus was walking along, in order to see Jesus. When Jesus came to the tree he looked up and said, "Zacchaeus, hurry down, I mean to stay at your house today." Zacchaeus quickly came down and welcomed Jesus with delight. The other people began to complain, "He has gone to a sinner's house as a guest."

Jesus said, "Today salvation has come to this house. The son of man [Jesus] has come to search out and save what was lost."

Stress
Zacchaeus was sorry. Jesus loved him, and forgave him. It is easy to point to someone else and say they did wrong like some of the people in today's story. But Zacchaeus said he was sorry for all he had done wrong. Jesus loved Zacchaeus for that and forgave him.

Activity
Sing the song "Zacchaeus" from "Joy Is like the Rain" record.

Matching cards from last week.

Liturgy
Gather around altar.

All pray together:
I will praise your name forever, my king and my God.
Jesus, I love you.
I will praise your name forever, my King and my God.
Jesus, I am sorry for any wrong I have done.
I will praise your name forever, my king and my God.
Jesus, thank you for loving me and forgiving me.
I will praise your name forever, my King and my God.

Letter to Parents
Dear Parents,
*   We are still learning about God's loving forgiveness. Continue to include an act of contrition and a thanksgiving for God's mercy in your family prayer time.*
*   Sincerely in Christ,*
*   Teacher _____*

Questions
Is it easy to blame someone else?
Should we admit our faults?
Should we say, "I am sorry"?
Will God forgive us when we say, "I am sorry"?

Cycle C
Thirty-second Sunday of Year

We Are God's Children

Supplies Needed
double-tipped swabs, two per student
variegated yarn, one piece two yards long per student

Activity
Begin by talking about what heaven means to each person present.

Lesson
Jesus told his friends that when we die and go to heaven, we will live there forever and never die again. We will be equal to the angels. We are children of God.

Liturgy
Gather around altar. Join hands.

All pray together:
Lord, when your glory appears, my joy will be full. Lord, one day I will live in heaven with you. You love me, Lord, and have made me your child. Lord, when your glory appears, my joy will be full.

Activity
Make the eye of God. Take home to hang in the bedroom to remind us that we are God's children. God loves us and watches over us.

To make: Tie yarn at center of swabs to form a cross. Wrap yarn around one leg of cross then next. Continue around all four legs until covered to cotton tips of swabs. Tie to fasten and prevent raveling. See diagram.

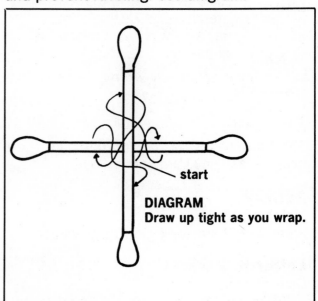

start

DIAGRAM
Draw up tight as you wrap.

Letter to Parents

Dear Parents,

We are God's children. God loves us. One day we will live in heaven with God. Include the psalm: "Lord, When Your Glory Appears, My Joy Will Be Full," in your family prayer this week.

Sincerely in Christ,
Teacher _____

Questions

Does God love us?
Is God our Father?
Are we God's children?
Does God watch over us?
Will we one day live in heaven with God?

Cycle C
Thirty-third Sunday of Year

We Thank God For Being Just

Supplies Needed

½ poster board per student
scissors
magazines
glue

(The gospel for this Sunday is of the destruction of Jerusalem and the end of the world. It is too frightening and difficult for the students. Today's lesson is based on the responsorial psalm for Sunday.)

Discuss

Thanksgiving and the things the students are thankful for. Stress the importance of thanking and praising God.

Lesson

The Lord comes to rule the earth with justice. Justice means being fair to others.

God sees into our hearts and understands better than anyone else why we do the things we do. God will be fair with us. This is God's justice. We thank God for being just and fair.

Liturgy

Gather around altar. Join hands.

All:

The Lord comes to rule the earth with justice. Thank you, Lord, for being just and fair. Thank you, Lord, for seeing into my heart and knowing me.
The Lord comes to rule the earth with justice.

Activity

Each student makes a collage of the things he/she is thankful for.

Letter to Parents

Dear Parents,

God sees into our hearts and knows us better than we know ourselves. In your prayers this week, thank God for his justice and understanding.

Sincerely in Christ,
Teacher _____

Questions

Does justice mean being fair?
Is God just and fair?
Should we thank God for being just and fair?

Cycle C
Thirty-fourth Sunday of Year

Because We Are Forgiven We Can One Day Go to Heaven

Supplies Needed

popsickle sticks, two per student
glue
pencils
small pieces of tissue paper in a variety of colors

Lesson

When Jesus was crucified [nailed to the cross] two thieves [robbers] were crucified with him, one on each side of him. One robber said to Jesus, "Lord, remember me when you get to heaven." (That was one way to tell Jesus he was sorry for his life of crime.)

Jesus said to him, "Today you will be with me in heaven."

Stress

Was the thief sorry? Did Jesus forgive him? When we say we are sorry to Jesus, he forgives us. Because we are forgiven we can one day go to heaven, as Jesus promised the thief when he was sorry.

Liturgy

Sit around altar. Close eyes.

All:
I rejoiced when I heard them say: Let us go to the house of the Lord.

Teacher:
Today when we say "Go to the house of the Lord" we think about going to heaven.

All:
I rejoiced when I heard them say: Let us go to the house of the Lord.

Teacher:
Let us quietly, in our hearts, ask Jesus to forgive us as he did the thief on the cross. (Pause.)

All:
I rejoiced when I heard them say: Let us go to the house of the Lord.

Activity

Make cross of flowers.

Glue two popsickle sticks in the form of a cross. Decorate with small tissue-paper flowers. Shape tissue paper over eraser end of pencil. Put glue on cross. Place shaped flowers into position. Completely cover cross.

Letter to Parents

Dear Parents,

Because we are forgiven we can one day go to heaven. In your prayers this week, include the psalm: "I Rejoiced When I Heard Them Say: Let Us Go to the House of the Lord."

Sincerely in Christ,
Teacher _____

Questions

Does Jesus forgive us when we say, "I am sorry"?
Will we go to heaven because we are forgiven?

Note to Teacher

Next week go to the First Sunday of Advent—Cycle A.